Bloom's BioCritiques

Dante Alighieri
Maya Angelou
Jane Austen
The Brontë Sisters
Lord Byron
Geoffrey Chaucer
Anton Chekhov
Stephen Crane
Emily Dickinson
William Faulkner
F. Scott Fitzgerald
Robert Frost
Ernest Hemingway
Langston Hughes
Stephen King
Arthur Miller
Toni Morrison
Edgar Allan Poe
J. D. Salinger
William Shakespeare
John Steinbeck
Mark Twain
Alice Walker
Walt Whitman
Tennessee Williams

Bloom's BioCritiques

EMILY DICKINSON

Edited and with an introduction by
Harold Bloom
Sterling Professor of the Humanities
Yale University

Philadelphia

A Haights Cross Communications Company

Printed and bound in the United States of America

10 9 8 7 6 5 4 3 2

Library of Congress Cataloging-in-Publication Data

Emily Dickinson / editor, Harold Bloom.
p. cm. — (Bloom's biocritiques)
ISBN 0-7910-6179-5 (hardcover) — ISBN 0-7910-7112-X (pbk.)
1. Dickinson, Emily, 1830-1886—Criticism and interpretation. I.
Bloom, Harold. II. Series.
PS1541.Z5 E37 2002
811'.4—dc21

2002009169

Chelsea House Publishers
1974 Sproul Road, Suite 400
Broomall, PA 19008-0914

http://www.chelseahouse.com

Contributing editor: Sandra McChesney

Cover design by Terry Mallon

Cover: ©Bettmann/CORBIS

Layout by EJB Publishing Services

CONTENTS

User's Guide

These volumes are designed to introduce the reader to the life and work of the world's literary masters. Each volume begins with Harold Bloom's essay "The Work in the Writer" and a volume-specific introduction also written by Professor Bloom. Following these unique introductions is an engaging biography that discusses the major life events and important literary accomplishments of the author under consideration.

Furthermore, each volume includes an original critique that not only traces the themes, symbols, and ideas apparent in the author's works, but strives to put those works into a cultural and historical perspective. In addition to the original critique is a brief selection of significant critical essays previously published on the author and his or her works followed by a concise and informative chronology of the writer's life. Finally, each volume concludes with a bibliography of the writer's works, a list of additional readings, and an index of important themes and ideas.

HAROLD BLOOM

The Work in the Writer

Literary biography found its masterpiece in James Boswell's *Life of Samuel Johnson.* Boswell, when he treated Johnson's writings, implicitly commented upon Johnson as found in his work, even as in the great critic's life. Modern instances of literary biography, such as Richard Ellmann's lives of W. B. Yeats, James Joyce, and Oscar Wilde, essentially follow in Boswell's pattern.

That the writer somehow is in the work, we need not doubt, though with William Shakespeare, writer-of-writers, we almost always need to rely upon pure surmise. The exquisite rancidities of the Problem Plays or Dark Comedies seem to express an extraordinary estrangement of Shakespeare from himself. When we read or attend *Troilus and Cressida* and *Measure for Measure*, we may be startled by particular speeches of Ulysses in the first play, or of Vincentio in the second. These speeches, of Ulysses upon hierarchy or upon time, or of Duke Vincentio upon death, are too strong either for their contexts or for the characters of their speakers. The same phenomenon occurs with Parolles, the military impostor of *All's Well That Ends Well.* Utterly disgraced, he nevertheless affirms: "Simply the thing I am/Shall make me live."

In Shakespeare, more even than in his peers, Dante and Cervantes, meaning always starts itself again through excess or overflow. The strongest of Shakespeare's creatures—Falstaff, Hamlet, Iago, Lear, Cleopatra—have an exuberance that is fiercer than their plays can contain. If Ben Jonson was at all correct in his complaint that "Shakespeare wanted art," it could have been only in a sense that he may not have intended. Where do the personalities of Falstaff or Hamlet touch a limit? What was it in Shakespeare that made the two parts of *Henry IV* and *Hamlet* into "plays unlimited"? Neither Falstaff nor Hamlet will be stopped: their wit, their beautiful, laughing speech, their intensity of being—all these are virtually infinite.

In what ways do Falstaff and Hamlet manifest the writer in the work? Evidently, we can never know, or know enough to answer with any authority. But what would happen if we reversed the question, and asked: How did the work form the writer, Shakespeare?

Of Shakespeare's inwardness, his biography tells us nothing. And yet, to an astonishing extent, Shakespeare created our inwardness. At the least, we can speculate that Shakespeare so lived his life as to conceal the depths of his nature, particularly as he rather prematurely aged. We do not have Shakespeare on Shakespeare, as any good reader of the Sonnets comes to realize: they do not constitute a key that unlocks his heart. No sequence of sonnets could be less confessional or more powerfully detached from the poet's self.

The German poet and universal genius, Goethe, affords a superb contrast to Shakespeare. Of Goethe's life, we know more than everything; I wonder sometimes if we know as much about Napoleon or Freud or any other human being who ever has lived, as we know about Goethe. Everywhere, we can find Goethe in his work, so much so that Goethe seems to crowd the writing out, just as Byron and Oscar Wilde seem to usurp their own literary accomplishments. Goethe, cunning beyond measure, nevertheless invested a rival exuberance in his greatest works that could match his personal charisma. The sublime outrageousness of the Second Part of *Faust*, or of the greater lyric and meditative poems, form a Counter-Sublime to Goethe's own daemonic intensity.

Goethe was fascinated by the daemonic in himself; we can doubt that Shakespeare had any such interests. Evidently, Shakespeare abandoned his acting career just before he composed *Measure for Measure* and *Othello*. I surmise that the egregious interventions by Vincentio and Iago displace the actor's energies into a new kind of mischief-making, a fresh opening to a subtler playwriting-within-the-play.

But what had opened Shakespeare to this new awareness? The answer is the work in the writer, *Hamlet* in Shakespeare. One can go further: it was not so much the play, *Hamlet*, as the character Hamlet, who changed Shakespeare's art forever.

Hamlet's personality is so large and varied that it rivals Goethe's own. Ironically Goethe's Faust, his Hamlet, has no personality at all, and is as colorless as Shakespeare himself seems to have chosen to be. Yet nothing could be more colorful than the Second Part of *Faust*, which is peopled by an astonishing array of monsters, grotesque devils, and classical ghosts.

A contrast between Shakespeare and Goethe demonstrates that in each—but in very different ways—we can better find the work in the person, than we can discover that banal entity, the person in the work. Goethe to many of his contemporaries, seemed to be a mortal god. Shakespeare, so far as we know, seemed an affable, rather ordinary fellow, who aged early and became somewhat withdrawn. Yet Faust, though Mephistopheles battles for his soul, is hardly worth the trouble unless you take him as an idea and not as a person. Hamlet is nearly every-idea-in-one, but he is precisely a personality and a person.

Would Hamlet be so astonishingly persuasive if his father's ghost did not haunt him? Falstaff is more alive than Prince Hal, who says that the devil haunts him in the shape of an old fat man. Three years before composing the final *Hamlet*, Shakespeare invented Falstaff, who then never ceased to haunt his creator. Falstaff and Hamlet may be said to best represent the work in the writer, because their influence upon Shakespeare was prodigious. W.H. Auden accurately observed that Falstaff possesses infinite energy: never tired, never bored, and absolutely both witty and happy until Hal's rejection destroys him. Hamlet too has infinite energy, but in him it is more curse than blessing.

Falstaff and Hamlet can be said to occupy the roles in Shakespeare's invented world that Sancho Panza and Don Quixote possess in Cervantes's. Shakespeare's plays from 1610 on (starting with *Twelfth Night*) are thus analogous to the Second Part of Cervantes's epic novel. Sancho and the Don overtly jostle Cervantes for authorship in the Second Part, even as Cervantes battles against the impostor who has pirated a continuation of his work. As a dramatist, Shakespeare manifests the work in the writer more indirectly. Falstaff's prose genius is revived in the scapegoating of Malvolio by Maria and Sir Toby Belch, while Falstaff's darker insights are developed by Feste's melancholic wit. Hamlet's intellectual resourcefulness, already deadly, becomes poisonous in Iago and in Edmund. Yet we have not crossed into the deeper abysses of the work in the writer in later Shakespeare.

No fictive character, before or since, is Falstaff's equal in self-trust. Sir John, whose delight in himself is contagious, has total confidence both in his self-awareness and in the resources of his language. Hamlet, whose self is as strong, and whose language is as copious, nevertheless distrusts both the self and language. Later Shakespeare is, as it were, much under the influence both of Falstaff and of Hamlet, but they tug him in opposite directions. Shakespeare's own copiousness of language is well-nigh incredible: a vocabulary in excess of twenty-one thousand words, almost eighteen hundred of which he coined himself. And of his word-hoard, nearly half are used only once each, as though the perfect setting for each had been found, and need not be repeated. Love for language and faith in language are Falstaffian attributes. Hamlet will darken both that love and that faith in Shakespeare, and perhaps the Sonnets can best be read as Falstaff and Hamlet counterpointing against one another.

Can we surmise how aware Shakespeare was of Falstaff and Hamlet, once they had played themselves into existence? *Henry IV*, *Part I* appeared in six quarto editions during Shakespeare's lifetime; *Hamlet* possibly had four. Falstaff and Hamlet were played again and again at the Globe, but Shakespeare knew also that they were being read, and he must have had contact with some of those readers. What would it have been like to discuss Falstaff or Hamlet with one of their early readers (presumably also part of their audience at the Globe), if you were the creator of such demiurges? The question would seem nonsensical to most Shakespeare scholars, but then these days they tend to be either ideologues or moldy figs. How can we recover the uncanniness of Falstaff and of Hamlet, when they now have become so familiar?

A writer's influence upon himself is an unexplored problem in criticism, but such an influence is never free from anxieties. The biocritical problem (which this series attempts to explore) can be divided into two areas, difficult to disengage fully. Accomplished works affect the author's life, and also affect her subsequent writings. It is simpler for me to surmise the effect of *Mrs. Dalloway* and *To the Lighthouse* upon Woolf's late *Between the Acts*, than it is to relate Clarissa Dalloway's suicide and Lily Briscoe's capable endurance in art to the tragic death and complex life of Virginia Woolf.

There are writers whose lives were so vivid that they seem sometimes to obscure the literary achievement: Byron, Wilde, Malraux, Hemingway. But most major Western writers do not live that exuberantly, and the greatest of all, Shakespeare, sometimes appears to have adopted the personal mask of colorlessness. And yet there are heroes of literature who struggled titanically with their own eras—Tolstoy, Milton, Victor Hugo—who nevertheless matter more for their works than their lives.

There are great figures—Emily Dickinson, Wallace Stevens, Willa Cather—who seem to have had so little of the full intensity of life when compared to the vitality of their work, that we might almost speak of the work in the work, rather than even of the work in a person. Emily Brontë might well be the extreme instance of such a visionary, surpassing William Blake in that one regard.

I conclude this general introduction to a series of literary bio-critiques by stating a tentative formula or principle for gauging the many ways in which the work influences the person and her subsequent, later work. Our influence upon ourselves is always related to the Shakespearean invention of self-overhearing, which I have written about in several other contexts. Life, as well as poetry and prose, is overheard rather than simply heard. The writer listens to herself as though she were somebody else, and the will to change begins to operate. The forces that live in us include the prior work we have done, and the dreams and waking visions that evade our dismissals.

HAROLD BLOOM

Introduction

Emily Dickinson's own poetry was the dominant influence upon the life she lived. Ultimately it counted for more than her complex and mostly repressed passional life, or her spiritual nimbleness in evading God and Immortality, or even the intricate familial relationship within and between the Dickinson households (her father Edward's and her brother Austin's).

Literary influences upon Dickinson inevitably include the Bible, Shakespeare, and Milton, and earlier in her own century, Wordsworth, Keats, Shelley and the Brownings. Yet the only influence worth her evading was that of Emerson: his poems sometimes are uncomfortably close to hers, and his program of metaphorical unnaming stimulated her own very rugged and independent poetic thinking. The Emersonian religion of Self-Reliance had an ambivalent effect upon Dickinson, whose family religious heritage was Calvinist, not Unitarian. The critic Allen Tate, always under the influence of T. S. Eliot, insisted that Dickinson had more of Hawthorne than of Emerson in her. That seems quite wrong to me, but I recall Tate telling me, each of the few times we met, that "Emerson was the Devil." This pronouncement was made so severely (as compared say to Robert Penn Warren's somewhat ironic identifications of the Devil and Ralph Waldo Emerson) that Tate meant it quite literally. But Emily Dickinson said of Emerson, who stayed overnight next door in her brother's house, that it was: "As if he had come from where dreams are born." Rather wickedly, she later asked:

"With the Kingdom of Heaven on his knee, could Mr. Emerson hesitate?"

I appropriate an observation I wrote somewhere decades ago: Dickinson is a heretic, whose only religion was Emersonianism, taking Emerson's doctrine as the exaltation of whim, which in Emerson (and Dickinson) has little to do with the whimsical. Far less dogmatically than Tate, James McIntosh has argued subtly for a residuum of Christian belief in Dickinson, but I am not persuaded. There are no limits to Dickinson's quite original kind of irony: "I am glad you love your Clergyman… God seems much more friendly through a hearty Lens." Still, McIntosh rightly emphasizes that Dickinson never maintains for long a single stance in relation to spiritual matters, any more than Thoreau or Melville do. These are all Post-Emersonian, and Emerson exalted transition and volatility. What Dickinson called a "waylaying Light" illuminated them all fitfully.

Emerson, as the late Sidney Ahlstrom observed, can be regarded as the theologian of "the American Religion," an extraordinary mixture of Orphic, Gnostic, and Enthusiastic strains that has prevailed in the United States for two centuries now, while still calling itself Protestantism. Dickinson, Walt Whitman, Hart Crane, and even the very secular Wallace Stevens are the very different poets who share this Native Strain. The overtly Emersonian Robert Frost stands apart from this faithless faith, even as Emerson does, though Emerson had first defined it. You can term Dickinson a "fundamentally religious poet," as McIntosh does, only if you disengage her religion from historical Protestantism. A belief in the permanence of the spirit need not be Christian (or Judaic, or Islamic). It is not Dickinson's Melvillean quarrel with God that much matters; whether or not Dickinson had a "project" is unknowable, but her passion for her own spiritual autonomy is enormous, and aligns her with the English High Romantic poets, and with Emerson. McIntosh usefully invokes William Blake, but her Eros places her closer to Shelley, and to Keats. She shares their visionary skepticism, and also their intimations of mortality.

Had Judge Otis Phillips Lord, who was of her father's generation, not sickened and died, Dickinson very likely would have married him. I find nothing in her poems or letters to indicate a lesbian passion for her sister-in-law Susan, Austin Dickinson's wife, though it is fashionable these days to surmise such a relationship. With Judge Lord, there is much more basis for speculation. Dickinson clearly had been in love with Samuel Bowles, but it was always a despairing love. Lord's wife died in December 1877; Samuel Bowles died the next month. From the summer of 1880 until Judge Lord's death in March 1884, Dickinson and the Judge appear to have had a love affair or intimate relationship. In summertime, 1880, Emily Dickinson was forty-nine, while Judge Lord was sixty-seven. About all they had in common (on the surface) was a mutual passion for Shakespeare, whom the Judge regarded as the god of common sense. It is certainly to Lord (whether before or after his death, we cannot know) that she addresses an extraordinary quatrain composed in 1844, numbered 1636 in R.W. Franklin's definitive edition of *The Poems of Emily Dickinson, Reading Edition* (1999):

Circumference thou Bride of Awe
Possessing thou shalt be
Possessed by every hallowed Knight
That dares—to Covet thee

"Awe" is one of her prime names for Judge Lord; "Circumference," here in particular, is Dickinson herself. The vaunting eroticism of this quatrain is confirmed by its overt allusion to a peak moment in Shelley's *Epipsychidion*, where the poet's beloved, Emilia Viviani, is addressed as "Emily":

Meanwhile
We two will rise, and sit, and walk together,
Under the roof of blue Ionian weather,
And wander in the meadows, or ascend
The mossy mountains, where the blue heavens bend
With lightest winds, to touch their paramour;
Or linger, where the pebble-paven shore,
Under the quick, faint kisses of the sea
Trembles and sparkles as with ecstasy,—
Possessing and possessed by all that is
Within that calm circumference of bliss,
And by each other, till to love and live
Be one: —

Dickinson brilliantly revises:

Possessing and possessed by all that is
Within that calm circumference of bliss

The major phase of Emily Dickinson's poetry had ended before her love affair with Otis Phillips Lord. Yet she returned to something like her full powers, as in poem 1653 (Franklin):

So give me back to Death–
The Death I never feared
Except that it deprived of thee–
And now, by Life deprived,
In my own Grave I breathe
And estimate it's size–
It's size is all that Hell can guess–
And all that Heaven was –

We may never know all we might concerning Dickinson's love for Bowles, or Lord, or perhaps sister-in-law Susan, but her vocation, writing poems, was her true election, her pragmatic religion, and—until very late—her Eros. Dickinson, who thought through everything for herself, to a degree comparable to Dante or Shakespeare, is a greater poet than as yet we know how to appreciate.

KAY CORNELIUS

Biography of Emily Dickinson

The Myth of Amherst

Emily Dickinson stands among the greatest poets produced by America and perhaps the English-speaking world. Her voice and verbal artistry are unique, and her themes are both ageless and universal. More than a hundred years after her death, Dickinson's ever-surprising phrasing and poignant observations seem startlingly "modern." No anthology of American poetry would be complete without the inclusion of her work, which continues to be read and enjoyed.

Dickinson's work, however, almost didn't survive her death. During her own lifetime, only a few of her poems were published, most of those without her consent. Had the poet's sister Lavinia followed Dickinson's request to have her documents burned, the bundles of papers found in a locked bureau drawer—a life's work of nearly two thousand poems—would have been lost. Lavinia Dickinson's rescue of these poems gave the world a great treasure.

Each new generation of students greets Dickinson's poems with delight and enthusiasm. Her poetry is so widely known that her name and likeness have made Dickinson a commercial marketing success. Sweatshirts, coffee mugs, and other objects with the familiar portrait taken when she was just seventeen sell briskly. By any measure, this woman who lived in seclusion and died in 1886 has become a literary celebrity. Despite Dickinson's ever-growing literary popularity, many details of her life remain a mystery. The most mundane facts of her existence have become shrouded in myth, wild suppositions, half-truths, and a few outright lies. In her own lifetime, she was an intensely private person who never sought—and would not have welcomed—the prying that comes with public acclaim. That great fame came after her death is a truth that the poet would find richly ironic. And although she did not actively seek an audience, some of Dickinson's poems seem to have anticipated one.

By 1862, Emily Dickinson had begun to conduct most of her life on her own terms and largely in private. That same year marked the first (and only) time that she had submitted any of her work for publication. Four poems were sent to Thomas Wentworth Higginson, a respected Boston editor, writer, and critic, who had written an article of advice and encouragement for young writers. He recognized the spark which inspired the poems, but they were so unlike the conventional poetry of the day that Higginson advised her not to seek immediate publication. However, he entered into a correspondence with Dickinson that continued until her death, after which Higginson was invited to help edit her work.

In one letter, in response to his request for her portrait, Dickinson wrote that she did not have one, but she described herself as "small, like the Wren, and my Hair is bold, like the Chestnut Burr—and my eyes, like the Sherry in the Glass, that the Guest leaves." When they finally did meet, several years later, Higginson described Dickinson to his wife as "a little plain woman with two small bands of reddish hair ... in a very plain and exquisitely clean white pique and a blue worsted shawl." In another letter to Higginson, Dickinson calls herself "the only Kangaroo among the Beauty," a remark that probably had more to do with the oddness of her poetry than her appearance.

As the years passed and Dickinson withdrew ever more from the activities and social life around her Amherst home, she became the subject of much gossip, occasioned by her "odd" behavior. Letters and diaries reveal that those who knew very little or nothing at all about her or the true circumstances of her life concluded that "Miss Emily" was eccentric, if not downright crazy. After all, they reasoned, there must be something very peculiar about a woman who never went anywhere, who refused to attend church or call on her neighbors, and who hid when visitors came to the home she shared with the rest of her family.

The very same gossips took Dickinson's dressing in white the year around as another sign that the elder daughter of the sensible and upright Squire Dickinson had become eccentric. She was a colorful character, the community gossips concluded, harmless enough, but definitely a bit peculiar. Her seclusion fit easily into the stereotypical role of the injured spinster and most likely provided fodder for countless speculations about her personal life.

The myth-making about Emily Dickinson that began in her lifetime has continued in the years since her death. As her poems and letters were discovered and made public, the inner life of the reclusive poet has become the subject of a great deal of speculation. A number of books and articles have appeared, resulting in many, often opposing, views of what the great poet was really like.

The search for the real Emily Dickinson—as opposed to "The Myth of Amherst"—is challenging. To further complicate the matter, much of the available evidence is open to more than one interpretation. Dickinson delighted in reading and writing riddles and in making metaphors, and it should not be surprising that she lived her life as such: concerned primarily with reading and writing.

The riddle that is Emily Dickinson is far from becoming "yesterday's surprise" any time soon. Despite the difficulties in distinguishing the facts from the fiction, a careful examination of her life and work yields helpful clues. Through them, some light can be shed on various aspects of her life, her personality, and her development as a powerful poet.

As with any individual, the time, the place, and even the atmosphere surrounding Emily Dickinson all influenced the ways she thought and acted and developed her natural talent. A line in one of her poems speaks of "seeing New Englandly," which proves an apt description for Dickinson's vision. What her Puritan background gave her and what of it she renounced are important keys to the shaping of her character.

Her education, both formal and informal, became an integral part of Dickinson and her writing. What she learned and read, what she thought of it, and how it might have influenced her are all important. It is known that during her year at South Hadley Seminary, she refused to join the Congregational church, and while she seems to have rejected traditional religious beliefs, her poems demonstrate a determined spiritual quest.

Another source of insight into Dickinson's life can be found at the Homestead, the house where she spent most of her life and in which she composed the main body of her work. The house still stands today and is open to the public as a museum. During its use, Emily shared it with the other members of the tightly-knit Dickinson family—her father, Edward; her mother, Emily Norcross; her older brother, William Austin; and her younger sister, Lavinia.

Next door to the Homestead stands the Evergreens, the home of Dickinson's brother Austin and his wife, Susan Gilbert Dickinson. Susan was Emily Dickinson's dearest friend and the one to whom she sent her first poetry. Austin and Susan's marriage was an unhappy one, and eventually dissolved after the death of eight-year-old Gilbert Dickinson, the couple's youngest son. The child's death profoundly affected the whole family, especially his Aunt Emily. Later, when Austin Dickinson fell in love with Mabel Loomis Todd—the woman who would later be asked to edit the poems Lavinia Dickinson found in her sister's room—their love affair became a scandal in Amherst. In addition to her family, Dickinson had many friends and acquaintances. Over the years, from the time she was a schoolgirl until her death, she continued to exchange short notes and regular letters (some many pages long) with a variety of both male and female correspondents. More than a thousand of these short writings have been gathered and published, providing yet another insight into the poet's life. Among the letters—including some that apparently were never sent—are several that seem to show that Dickinson was, indeed, deeply in love at least once in her life.

There also exist the poems themselves: the extraordinary hidden store of 1,775 that Lavinia Dickinson discovered after her sister's death. The poet's distinctive but hard-to-read handwriting and her untraditional punctuation, or lack of it, have presented problems to nearly every scholar who has attempted to edit them for publication. It took many years and a disastrous family feud before Thomas H. Johnson gathered all of the known poems together in one volume. In his editing (used throughout this piece), Johnson tried to reproduce the poems as closely as possible to how they were originally written. In addition, he took great efforts to give the poems approximate dates. Finally, instead of using titles, which with a very few exceptions Dickinson never did, Johnson numbered the poems.

These poems show not just one Emily Dickinson but several—sometimes writing as an irreverent little girl while at others writing as a grief-stricken, mature woman. Some poems reveal the poet to be a keen and admiring observer of nature, whereas in others she appears to be indifferent. And while she writes stirringly about heaven and immortality, it is seldom phrased in conventional religious terms.

Dickinson is, like much of her writing, a paradox; a complex and gifted writer who early determined to meet life on her own terms. Several of her poems speak of the beauty in Truth, but she also knew the danger that sometimes accompanies telling it. In one poem (1129), she writes:

> Tell all the Truth but tell it slant—
> Success in Circuit lies
> Too bright for our infirm Delight
> The Truth's superb surprise
>
> As Lightning to the Children eased
> With explanation kind
> The Truth must dazzle gradually—
> Or every man be blind—

Whatever "truths" are to be found about Emily Dickinson, a good place to start the search is her heritage, the background that framed the life of the family into which she was born on December 10, 1830.

"Puritans All"

Emily Dickinson apparently cared little for the study of genealogy, yet she was fully aware that her family tree had its roots deep in a Puritan heritage that went back seven generations before her birth. In all that time, no Dickinson man had ever taken a wife from outside New England.

The American Dickinson family traces its line from Nathaniel Dickinson, who came from England to Massachusetts with other Puritans in the Great Migration of 1630. Puritanism as a movement was started early in the sixteenth century by Protestant reformers who aimed to "purify" religion and politics. While the word "Puritan" was originally used to mock the movement, the group adopted the name for themselves as a badge of honor. Despite the continued efforts of Elizabeth I to move England into Protestantism, the Puritans believed that she was not doing enough to rid the country of Catholic influences. Furthermore, in emphasizing the importance of an individual's personal relationship with God, the Puritans wished to eliminate all distracting decoration from the church, including music, stained-glass windows, incense, and robes for clergymen—thus allowing the members of the congregation to properly concentrate on the state of their own spirituality.

As a result of the Puritans' criticism of England's established church, they were severely persecuted. In 1630, a group of Puritans under the leadership of John Winthrop sailed to Massachusetts Bay on a ship called the *Arabella*. They thought of New England as a place where they could establish a church and state government based on the laws of God (a "theocracy") that would serve as a model of reform for England and other parts of the world. It was to be as Winthrop described " ... that men shall say of succeeding plantations: the lord make it like that of New England: for we must Consider that we shall be as a City upon a Hill, the eyes of all people are upon us ..."

Many of the Puritans' religious doctrines came from the writings of the Protestant reformer John Calvin. He believed in predestination, and that good Puritans had to examine their lives daily for signs of God's disfavor. To help them develop their faith, they relied on the Bible; *The New England Primer*, from which generations of Dickinsons learned their letters; and *The Bay Psalm Book*, from which came the meter that Emily Dickinson used in many of her poems.

One famous Puritan minister was Jonathan Edwards, whose sermon "Sinners in the Hands of an Angry God" emphasizes the total depravity of man and the necessity for personal salvation. Other characteristics of Puritanism included thrift, which at times bordered on miserliness, hard work, and practicality. They wasted nothing, including words. Except for the ministers' sermons, which were often long and usually elegant, New Englanders were not known as great talkers.

The Puritans found it difficult to maintain the kind of "earthly paradise" they had hoped to form. Over the years, some members of the group left for other parts of New England. In 1659, because of a church split, Nathaniel Dickinson and 58 other men and their families moved to the new plantation of Hadley near Northampton, Massachusetts.

Nathaniel Dickinson was a town leader whose grandson, Ebenezer Dickinson, fought with Indians at Deerfield after the Massacre of 1704. In 1745, Ebenezer's son, Nathan, and grandson, Nathan, Jr., moved into the district that in 1759 was to become Amherst. In 1775, Nathan, Jr.'s, son, Samuel Fowler Dickinson, Emily's grandfather, was born.

Until Emily's grandfather's time, the numerous Dickinsons had been solid citizens who farmed for a living. Like all Puritans, they believed in the value of education so that each individual could read and study the scriptures. But with Samuel Fowler Dickinson, attaining a good education became more important. He entered Dartmouth College when he was sixteen and graduated second in his class. After brief tries at teaching school and being a minister, he turned to the law and became a distinguished member of that profession. In 1802 he married Lucretia Gunn, with whom he had five children. The eldest, Edward Dickinson, was born in 1803. Ten years later, Samuel Fowler Dickinson built the first brick dwelling in Amherst. An imposing house on Main Street, "the Homestead" would be Emily Dickinson's home for most of her life.

Samuel Fowler Dickinson's greatest achievement, the founding of Amherst College, was also the cause of his downfall. The original purpose of the school was to civilize and evangelize the world by providing young men of piety and talents with a classical education. To that end, its founders rejected the liberalism they saw in Harvard, which had become increasingly secular, as had some of the church congregations started by staunch Puritans.

Samuel Fowler Dickinson put so much of his time, energy, and money into the building of the college that both his health and law practice failed under the strain. He was forced to sell the Homestead in 1833 and to accept a position at a college in Cincinnati. In addition to his health problems, Samuel Fowler Dickinson apparently suffered a mental breakdown. He died in 1838 at the age of 63, far from the place and much of the family he loved. Of his children, only Edward Dickinson, Samuel Fowler Dickinson's eldest son, stayed in Amherst.

After attending Amherst College for one year, Edward Dickinson went to Yale University, where he apparently made many friends and decided to enter the legal profession.

In 1826 he met Emily Norcross, a quiet, amiable young woman from nearby Monson who seemed to embody all the traits that Edward Dickinson wanted in a wife. In the letter in which he proposed marriage to her, Edward Dickinson wrote, "My life must be a life of business, of labor and application to the study of my profession."

Two months before the wedding, he added, "Let us prepare for a life of rational happiness. I do not expect, neither do I desire a life of *pleasure*, as some call it—I anticipate pleasure from engaging with my whole soul in my business … and with my dearest friend.… May we be happy, useful & successful."

Edward Dickinson might not always have been happy—his portrait tends to make him look as if he suffered from severe indigestion—but by any measure he was both useful and successful. In addition to his private law practice, Edward Dickinson was elected to be Moderator of the Amherst Town Meeting for sixteen years. In 1835 he became the Treasurer of the school his father had helped to start, serving in that capacity for thirty-seven years, during which time Amherst College never lost money. No doubt Edward Dickinson felt that he had in some measure made up for his father's financial failure.

Another of Edward Dickinson's projects was aimed at bringing the railroad to Amherst, not for any personal gain on his part, but because he thought it would bring more prosperity to the area. Like his father before him, Edward excelled in public speaking; unlike his father, however, Edward seemed to be able to balance all the demands placed on him. In addition to his law practice and work at Amherst, Edward Dickinson served in the Massachusetts House and Senate and the United States House of Representatives. As a lawyer, he was admitted to practice before the Supreme Court, and he was also asked to run for lieutenant governor of Massachusetts.

Although Amherst College had been founded by men who thought that other colleges had become weak on Puritanism, the fact was that by Emily Dickinson's time, the ardent Puritanism of a few generations earlier had become diluted. The Puritan virtues of simplicity, austerity, hard work, and denial of the flesh remained, but the work that should have been done for God's glory was often given over to earthly ambition. The result was that many people who claimed to be pious were actually hypocrites. Instead of renouncing Puritanism's stern tenets, many people lived in a perpetual state of guilt and anguish.

The Connecticut Valley, where Amherst is located, underwent at least eight revivals between 1840 and 1860 in which people were called to search their souls, confess their sins, and repent. Emily Dickinson was ten years old when the first of these revivals swept Amherst, and she was thirty during the last. They caused her great anguish, because she did not see herself as one of the sinners whom Jonathan Edwards described vividly.... Dickinson could never testify, as so many others did, that she had received the direct visitation of the Spirit that was essential to membership in the church. However, the fact that she could not always be completely comfortable in rejecting the revivalists' pleas affirmed her Puritan heritage.

As was the Puritan custom, Dickinson continually examined her inner life, engaging in a kind of dialogue with herself that forms the basis of some of her finest poetry. The way of thinking that seemed so natural to her had its roots in a Puritanism that still influences American life today.

Dickinson knew what the Puritan traits were. She recognized them in herself and in her family, but she was always critical of them. Scholar Allen Tate claims that Dickinson lived during an ideal time for a poet, when the once mighty and firm tradition of Puritanism was losing its vitality and opening new freedoms for her. Sometimes this freedom was exhilarating; at other times, it terrified her.

Not being bound to traditional ways of thought that fettered others also meant that Dickinson lacked the security that they enjoyed. She often used the metaphor of the voyage to describe her feelings. In a letter to a pious friend written when she was twenty, Dickinson proclaimed, "The shore is safer, but I love to buffet the sea ... I love the danger!"

Despite that declaration, Edward Dickinson's daughter began her educational journey in the safest of all waters as she embarked on the years of study that would shape her thought for the rest of her life.

"Improving the Mind"

In the general population of nineteenth century America, education was sometimes a hit-or-miss proposition. The belief that all children should be entitled to a free education was more often an ideal than a reality. Even in a state like Massachusetts with a strong Puritan background that emphasized the necessity for education on religious grounds, the quality of free and universal education varied from place to place. Almost everywhere, the education of women was a distant second to that of men.

In the Dickinson household of Amherst, however, this was not the case. Edward Dickinson understood the benefits of education, not only for his son but also for his daughters. His advice to them, in a letter written when Emily was seven, shows a Puritan father's view:

> My Dear Little Children, Your mother writes me that you have been quite good since I came away.... I

> want to have you grow up & become good men & women and learn all you can, so that you can teach others to do right.... All you learn, now, when you are young, will do you a great deal of good, when you are grown up.

Emily Dickinson started her education when she was about five years old in the West Middle District School, where children of several ages were taught in the same room. In this primary school she learned the basics of reading, writing, and arithmetic. However, the opening of her mind to the world about her began in earnest when Emily Dickinson entered Amherst Academy in September of 1840.

Amherst Academy was a private school that had opened in 1812 with Noah Webster, the dictionary-maker, and Emily's own grandfather, Samuel Fowler Dickinson, among the members of the Board of Trustees. Seven years later, the same men founded Amherst College, and that school's graduates and teachers provided a ready source of good instructors for the pupils at the Amherst Academy.

Emily and Lavinia enrolled in the "English course." Richard B. Sewall's *The Life of Emily Dickinson* states that according to the Academy, its pupils "will be allowed to attend Lectures in the College, on History, Chemistry and Natural Philosophy." Prayer was a part of the daily routine, and pupils were expected to "attend on the public worship of God on the sabbath."

Among the lecturers at both Amherst College and Amherst Academy was Edward Hitchcock, a scientist who also had the soul of a poet. He intended to lead his students to God by the study of works of nature. In addition to classroom lectures, he conducted field trips to explore the botany and geology of the area, taking along his students and other young people from the town.

According to Sewall's *The Life of Emily Dickinson*, she delighted in finding and labeling plants. Dickinson enjoyed making a "herbarium," a book consisting of pressed flowers and other plants, each carefully labeled with its Latin name. In 1842 she wrote a friend, "besides Latin I study History and Botany." Three years later she wrote in another letter that she was studying "Mental Philosophy, Geology, Latin and Botany.... We have a very fine school."

Although Hitchcock was responsible primarily for his students' scientific education, his Puritanism also led him to warn them of the dangers of reading literature produced by atheists, such as Voltaire, or men of "low principle," such as Shakespeare. Edward Dickinson also endorsed such sentiments, and so his children had to smuggle novels and poetry into the house that might not have passed their father's test of "fitness."

Each Wednesday afternoon, students had exercises in composition and declamation (making speeches). In 1842, Dickinson entered "The Classical Department" and began to study Latin and Greek texts, including the Greek Testament. Her work also continued in mathematics, geography, ancient history and English grammar and composition.

In addition to her academic studies, Dickinson took music lessons and practiced playing the piano, at which she was apparently quite proficient. She also learned to perform the multitude of tasks necessary for the smooth running of a household. Cleaning, dusting, and scrubbing never appealed to her, but she enjoyed baking bread and making gingerbread and special desserts for the family.

As generations of girls had done before her, Dickinson embroidered a sampler as evidence that she had learned the basics of needlework. That sampler, now displayed in the Houghton Library in Amherst, also indicates why she wasn't renowned for her sewing skills.

Dickinson also learned some hard lessons about the brevity of life. In April 1844 her friend and second cousin Sophia Holland died. Dickinson's grief was so great that her worried parents sent her to Monson for a month's visit with her Aunt Lavinia Norcross in the hope that a change of scene would ease her melancholy....

Then, in 1848, Leonard Humphrey, who had been principal of the Academy in 1846–1848 and whom Emily considered a friend, died after a brief illness. She wrote her friend Abiah Root, "my master has gone to rest ... the tears come, and I cannot brush them away; I would not if I could, for they are the only tribute I can pay the departed Humphrey."

The twin subjects of death and immortality would occupy Dickinson for her entire life; she wrote poem after poem about those great mysteries.

Dickinson's final term at the Academy ended on August 10, 1847. Whereas most New Englanders would have agreed that an Amherst Academy education was sufficient for a girl, Edward Dickinson wanted to give his daughters more. He determined that Emily, and later her sister Lavinia, would be sent away to receive the nearest thing that passed for a university education for women in those days.

South Hadley Seminary, more widely known as Mount Holyoke, was an established school with a good reputation that had been in operation for ten years. A ninety-minute carriage ride from Amherst, the Seminary was hardly at the ends of the earth. But except for short visits to the Norcross relatives in nearby Monson, Dickinson had never before been this far away from home, and she had never spent a night under a roof that didn't belong to a family member.

Despite the knowledge that she would probably become homesick, Dickinson looked forward to the intellectual stimulation of further education. The school year consisted of two terms of five months each, and the student body was divided into junior, middle, and senior classes. On September 30, 1847, Dickinson entered the junior class, hoping to be able to qualify for the middle class after a short time.

The school's founder, Mary Lyon, intended that the young women who came under its influence would contribute to the good of society. Like Lyon, many writers and educators in Dickinson's time believed that women's special mission was to improve the nation by being a good moral influence on the home and community.

In many ways, Lyon was a unique female role model for her students. Like Dickinson, she had been a student at Amherst Academy and later studied science with Edward Hitchcock. When Lyon began to plan a school for the higher education of women, Hitchcock encouraged her and helped in the planning. Like Hitchcock, Lyon was both a scientist and a spiritual leader. She taught chemistry and always (as one of her colleagues wrote) impressed on her pupils' minds "the power, wisdom, and goodness of God, as displayed in his works."

"We have great power over ourselves. We may become almost what we will," Lyon told her students. Such a statement sounds harmless enough now, but to Emily Dickinson and the other young women of her time, Lyon's words were both revolutionary and energizing. Even if no one would ever say so out loud, young women of those days had been brought up to rely on men to shape the way they thought of themselves. First fathers, then brothers, and finally husbands made all the important decisions for the girls and women in their families. They also owned all of the property and made the financial decisions that affected the families.

Years later, when Dickinson wrote, "I took my Power in my Hand," she was following Lyon's example.

Another of Lyon's injunctions to her students also gave Dickinson pause for thought: "Never write a foolish thing in a letter or elsewhere," she warned. Dickinson would express this similar thought in Poem 1212:

A word is dead
When it is said,
Some say.
I say it just
Begins to live
That day.

In true Puritan fashion, daily self-examination was required of all Seminary students. The long list of rules included one that specified each girl should report her own transgressions, which would result in "black marks" on her record. Pupils were not to be late or absent from classes and meals. They could not speak above a whisper in halls and while working. They were not to sit on their beds or to visit other rooms without permission.

Each student was also expected to work. The school had no hired help, and the staff and pupils did everything that was needed, from cooking to cleaning. In comparison with her chores at home, Dickinson's duty assignment must have seemed easy. She collected and washed knives from the first tier of tables in the dining hall and then returned them to the proper place for the next meal.

Dickinson also enjoyed a compatible roommate. Emily Norcross was her first cousin (both girls were named for Dickinson's mother) and had long been a friend as well. As young girls, they might have worked on their samplers together, inasmuch as both chose the same verse of scripture.

In her superior education at the Amherst Academy, Dickinson had already studied many of the texts taught to the junior class. However, not all of her instruction was academic. In one letter, Dickinson told her brother, "We are furnished with an account-book, here & obliged to put down every mill, which we spend & what we spend for it & show it to Miss Whitman every Saturday, so you perceive your sister is learning to keep accounts in addition to the other branches of her education."

In addition to training their minds, Lyon believed that it was her duty to give all her charges the opportunity to become professed Christians by the time they left her school, if they had not already done so. The 300 students were divided into groups, depending on their spiritual state. The first group consisted of those who had already been converted and were professing Christians. In the second group were those who had "some hope" of conversion, while the third had "no hope" of conversion at all.

Dickinson was assigned to the last group and stayed there, despite daily exhortations from Lyon and others to save her soul. There seemed to be times when she was on the brink of joining the ranks of the converted, but she never did, despite the urging of Lyon, whom Dickinson greatly admired.

In addition to the worrisome emphasis on her spiritual condition, Dickinson also experienced homesickness and physical illness. At the close of the first term in January of 1848, when Edward Dickinson came to bring her home to Amherst for the two-week vacation, he must have been disturbed that his daughter looked so thin and pale. Without asking his daughter's opinion, he decided that she should return to South Hadley Seminary for the rest of that term but that she wouldn't return there the next year. In February, for the first time in her life, Dickinson didn't take part in the week-long celebration in which valentines were sent and received. She had always enjoyed sending satirical essays and highly original verses to her friends, but Lyon didn't approve of such foolishness, and her charges were forbidden to send or receive valentines. Dickinson wrote her brother, "Probably, Mary, Abby & Viny (Lavinia) have received scores of them from the infatuated wights in the neighborhood while your *highly accomplished & gifted elder sister* is entirely overlooked."

The next month brought the dreaded midterm examinations, made even worse by the fact that pupils were examined orally and in public, whereby anyone who wanted to attend was invited to come and listen. Never fond of any examination, Emily Dickinson spent many long hours reviewing her studies. She caught a bad cold that grew steadily worse, and when her friend Abby Wood came to visit her the week after examinations, Abby reported the state of Emily's health to her father. Despite his daughter's protests, Edward Dickinson sent Austin to bring Emily home to Amherst. She kept up with her studies as well as she could, but it was six weeks before she was allowed to return to South

Hadley Seminary. Of the experience, she said, "Father is quite a hand to give medicine, especially if it is not desirable to the patient, and I was dosed for about a month after my return home, without any mercy, till at last out of mere pity my cough went away, and I had quite a season of peace."

While she was at home, Emily Dickinson made an important new friend in Benjamin Franklin Newton, who was studying law in her father's office. Newton had read the popular novels and poems of the day and led her to read Longfellow's *Evangeline* and Tennyson's *The Princess*. She also read several novels before returning to school for the last term.

In early August after South Hadley Academy held its closing exercises, Dickinson left it, and her formal education, behind, apparently with no regrets. In addition to her schoolwork, she had learned several other valuable lessons. After living more or less on her own for a year, she had gained valuable insights into self-examination and living a disciplined life, both of which were necessary to her development as a poet.

But at that time, Dickinson's greatest feeling was pure relief that she would at last be back at the place she loved the most: her Amherst home.

"Home Sweet Home"

Dickinson eagerly returned to Amherst and to the house on North Pleasant Street, where the Dickinsons had lived for the past eight years. It was a rather plain two-story white frame dwelling that adjoined the village graveyard. From a north window, the family could watch funeral processions enter the main gates of the cemetery.

Her home, always the center of Dickinson's life, seemed even more precious after her return from South Hadley Seminary. Dickinson had liked the girls she met when she was away at school but had found none she cared for as much as she did her Amherst friends. In addition to Abby Wood, Abiah Root, Mary Warner, and Emily Fowler, whom she had known all her life, Dickinson also met Susan Gilbert. A native of Amherst who had been living with relatives in New York for some time, Susan Gilbert returned to Amherst about the same time that Dickinson came home from the South Hadley Seminary. The young women shared a common bond. Both had a ready wit and a shared enthusiasm for the sort of "worldly" literature that Edward Dickinson so distrusted.

With her friends, both male and female, Emily Dickinson enjoyed many social activities. In the summer, they went on picnics. In winter, they enjoyed sleigh rides and candy scrapes. "Sugaring off" maple trees was a favorite pastime, as were walking and going for carriage rides. Indoor activities included a Shakespeare reading club and playing charades. The girls often played and sang in impromptu musicales. Among the tunes that the Dickinson girls played were some "quick steps." They also sang popular ballads such as "Home Sweet Home."

Even though she had always been naturally shy and retiring, Emily Dickinson felt comfortable around her friends, and they delighted in her fine mind and quick repartee. One of the young men with whom Dickinson enjoyed matching wits was George Gould. In 1850, she sent him a long nonsense valentine full of "classical Latin" references, many of which she had made up. Gould published her valentine anonymously in the Amherst literary magazine, which he edited at the time.

Dickinson's first published piece begins, "Magnum bonum,'harum scarum,' zounds et zounds, et war alarum, man reformam, life perfectum, mundum changum, all things flarum?" and goes on to claim that its writer is "Judith the heroine of the Apocrypha…. That's what they call a metaphor in our country. Don't be afraid of it, sir, it won't bite. If it was my *Carlo* now!"

Although her name was not attached, few readers would fail to recognize its author. The reference to Carlo, the Newfoundland dog that Dickinson's father presented to his daughter for protection when she roamed about the woods, would have given Dickinson away even if the spirited and high-flown language did not. The dog remained Dickinson's constant companion for the next fifteen years, as one after another her Amherst friends fell away.

Newton, nearly ten years older than Dickinson, was never part of her social set. However, her father's law clerk continued to influence and shape her literary tastes. He introduced Dickinson to the writing of the Brontë sisters, for which she had great enthusiasm. He also gave her a copy of the poems of Ralph Waldo Emerson, who had yet to become famous in American literature. Their discussions ranged widely, from politics and religion to poetry. Dickinson had begun to try writing a few verses, which she showed to Newton. He praised them and urged her to do better. Perhaps for the first time, Dickinson began to believe that she could become a poet.

Newton left Amherst in 1849 to open a law practice in Worcester and married two years later, but he and Dickinson continued a correspondence that meant a great deal to her. His death from consumption in March of 1853 was another great loss, coming as it did soon after the death of her cousin Emily Norcross, her South Hadley Seminary roommate.

Months later, Dickinson wrote to Newton's minister in Worcester, asking about his state of mind and willingness to die. Dickinson called Newton "the friend who taught her immortality but himself ventured too near."

Without Newton's guidance, Dickinson had only her "Lexicon" (dictionary) to rely upon as she continued to write poetry.

In the first few years after Dickinson returned to Amherst, the three Dickinson siblings were seldom all home at the same time. Austin went away for further education at Harvard, which was followed by a brief tenure of teaching school in Boston. In 1850, Lavinia ("Vinnie") went away to Ipswich Seminary for two terms, the same amount of time that Emily had spent at South Hadley Seminary. While her brother and sister were away, Emily wrote to them often. Her lively letters related local happenings and always mentioned how much she missed them.

The Dickinson siblings got along together well and genuinely enjoyed one another's company. However, Austin and Emily Dickinson felt closer to one another than either did to Lavinia. Each of Edward and Emily Norcross Dickinson's three children had distinctive personalities. They also varied in appearance. Austin was tall; Emily was petite. Both had red hair; Austin's was "unruly," whereas Emily wore hers pulled back from her face and confined in a net. Emily considered herself "plain," but her few likenesses show even features and striking eyes. Lavinia's pictures reveal that she had a pretty face and dark, wavy hair.

Austin and Emily Dickinson shared a deep interest in and love for nature. Both studied botany with Edward Hitchcock at the Amherst Academy, but even before that, as young children Austin and Emily had taken long, rambling walks through the woods and meadows around Amherst. They searched for wildflowers in the spring and summer months and gathered nuts in the fall. Later in his life, Austin Dickinson led a drive to landscape the long-neglected Amherst Commons. He took great pride in the plantings around his own home, as did Emily, who gardened and grew exotic plants.

The two also shared a love of books and reading, and they often conspired together to obtain and read works disapproved by their father. When Austin was gone, Emily once told him in a letter that the house was too quiet. She had "nobody to laugh with—talk with, nobody down in the morning to make the fun for me!"

As the family beauty, Lavinia had her share of suitors. She was as capable of being witty as her brother and sister, but she had a sharp manner of speaking that grew more pronounced as she aged. She was certainly intelligent, but even though she and her sister had a similar education, Lavinia wanted to pursue matters of the mind. In that respect, she resembled their mother.

"Mother does not care for thought," was the way Emily Dickinson once put it. Although Emily Norcross Dickinson had been well educated for her time, she apparently agreed with the commonly held belief that her only important roles were to care for her husband and children first and then to extend her charity to their neighbors and the town's needy. She called on newcomers and the ill, and once each year she opened the Dickinson home for a gala reception after Amherst College's commencement ceremonies. She knew her duty and did it to the best of her ability; anything else would have been frivolous and unseemly.

In her portrait as a young woman, Emily Norcross's calm demeanor seems to proclaim an inner peace. Edward Dickinson courted Emily Norcross a long time. Unlike her sister Lavinia, who married a cousin "for love" against the wishes of her parents, Emily Norcross seems to have weighed Edward Dickinson in the balance before agreeing to become his wife.

As might be expected for a woman in her position, Emily Norcross Dickinson proved to be a good housewife. She excelled in cooking and baking, skills that her daughter Emily mastered so well that Lavinia was more than willing to leave the desserts and bread making to her sister. Their mother's love of flowers and cultivation of a fine garden gave mother and daughter a shared bond. However, they were not close.

From the time of Lavinia's birth, Mrs. Dickinson had experienced spells of poor health. When she took to her bed, sometimes for days at a time, it was up to the girls to keep the household functioning. Only in her later years when Mrs. Dickinson became an invalid and her daughters had her complete care did Emily really learn to love her mother.

Neither Austin Dickinson nor his sisters seemed to have much concern about their parents when they were in their teenage and young adult years, except as they affected the things they wanted to do. When Austin was away, both sisters sent him letters. Emily wrote Austin that she would leave all matters of fact to practical Lavinia and write her brother only the interesting things.

Early on, the rest of the family learned that Lavinia could be depended upon to see to the practical matters of the household. Once, Emily wrote Austin that they had cleaned house all week: "—that is to say, Mother and Vinnie did, and I scolded, because they moved my things—I cant find much left anywhere, that I used to wear, or know of. You will easily conclude that I am surrounded by trial."

Like her older sister, Lavinia Dickinson never married, although she came close to becoming engaged on several occasions. At least once, her father's disapproval ended the matter; in another case, she apparently refused a proposal from someone she didn't care for enough to leave her home. In addition to seeing that the household ran smoothly, Lavinia also became the buffer between the world and her family. Anyone who criticized a Dickinson family member did so in peril of Lavinia's sharp tongue.

Emily Dickinson depended on her sister for practical things, but perhaps even more important were Lavinia's companionship and loyalty. When Lavinia spent one winter in Boston taking care of a Norcross aunt, Emily Dickinson wrote a friend: "I would like more sisters, that the taking out of one, might not leave such stillness. Vinnie has been all, so long, I feel the oddest fright at parting with her for an hour, lest a storm arise, and I go unsheltered."

When Lavinia was at the Ipswich Seminary, she became caught up in the same sort of revival fervor that had swept South Hadley Seminary when Emily was there. In a fervent letter to Austin, she pleaded that he and Emily might give themselves to Christ as she had done. Amherst, in both the college and the town, was also undergoing yet another of the great revivals that regularly swept through it. Emily Dickinson's friends Abby Wood, Mary Warner, Jane Humphrey, and Susan Gilbert all publicly announced their conversions.

Once more, Dickinson felt unable to join them: "one of the lingering *bad* ones, and so do *I* slink away, and pause, and ponder, and ponder, and pause, and do work without knowing why." However, Edward Dickinson, who had been an active and pious churchgoer all his life, took the conversion message to heart and was among the 70 persons (including Susan Gilbert) who joined the church as a result of the revival.

This late coming into the flock was only one of Edward Dickinson's sometimes surprising, even contradictory, acts. Stern and rigid Puritan that he was, his behavior was usually predictable. But at times he did things that seemed to be totally out of character.

One evening the people of Amherst heard the church bell pealing frantically, the usual signal that something was on fire. They rushed outside to see what was burning, only to be treated to a beautifully colored display of the aurora borealis (northern lights), courtesy of Edward Dickinson's desire to share the magnificent sight.

Emily was Edward Dickinson's favorite daughter. Even when their strong wills collided, Emily knew how to manage her father. One day when Edward Dickinson complained that the same nicked plate was always set before him, Emily carried the plate outside and broke it into pieces on a stone "just to remind" her, as she put it, not to give it to her father again.

In response to a question about her family in 1862, Emily wrote of her Father that he is ... "too busy with his Briefs—to notice what we do—He buys me many Books—but begs me not to read them—because he fears they joggle the Mind. They are religious—except me—and address an Eclipse, every morning—whom they call their 'Father.'"

As is often the case with such men, Edward Dickinson was both devoted to and dependent on his family, yet he seemed unable to speak of his love for them. At times he must have wondered how his children could have turned out to be so different from their parents.

Once Emily Dickinson wrote a friend, "My father seems to me often the oldest and oddest sort of a foreigner. Sometimes I say something and he stares in a curious sort of bewilderment though I speak a thought quite as old as his daughter...."

Austin Dickinson and his father argued quite often when they were together, but when Austin went away, his father eagerly awaited his letters. Emily wrote to Austin that their father read all the letters he wrote as soon as he picked them up from the post office, no matter to whom Austin addressed them, "... then he makes me read them loud at the supper table again, and when he gets home in the evening, he cracks a few walnuts, puts his spectacles on, and with your last in hand, sits down to enjoy the evening."

Edward Dickinson was serving a second term in Congress in 1855 when, with Austin at Harvard Law School, Lavinia and Emily Dickinson traveled to Washington for a three-week visit with their father. It was the farthest Emily ever traveled from Amherst, and her letters from Washington indicate how glad she would be to get back home.

However, before returning to Amherst, Edward Dickinson accompanied his daughters to Philadelphia on March 4. There Emily apparently met Charles Wadsworth, a powerful Presbyterian minister. Nothing is known about their meeting or what each thought of the other, but he must have left an impression as she later began a correspondence with the minister that lasted until Wadsworth's death. She probably first wrote to Wadsworth after reading his sermons, at a time in her life when her mother's illness weighed heavily upon her. When Wadsworth died in 1882, letters to mutual acquaintances show that she cared deeply for him.

A highly romantic version says that Dickinson fell in love with Wadsworth, who was already married, and that her inability to be with the man she loved was the tragic circumstance that made her withdraw from social activities and inspired her love poems.

Wadsworth visited Amherst in 1869, two years before he accepted a call to preach in a church in San Francisco, and again in 1880. Whether he was merely a spiritual advisor who helped her resolve her questions about religion, death and immortality, or something more, Wadsworth played an important role in her life. He was not the only man who would do so, but when she returned from Washington, Dickinson had many other things to occupy her mind, including changes in her residence and in the makeup of her family.

The Homestead and the Evergreens

Neither Lavinia nor Emily Dickinson ever married, but their brother Austin fell in love with Emily's friend Susan Gilbert before he finished law school in 1854. After a long and at times stormy courtship, Susan finally agreed to marry him. Austin wanted to relocate to Chicago and establish a law practice in that thriving city. Apparently, Susan had no objections but, predictably, his plan was not acceptable to Edward Dickinson. Austin's father liked Susan Gilbert well enough (and even Lavinia approved of her), but Edward Dickinson wanted his son to live in Amherst.

After buying back the old Dickinson homestead and 13 acres around it on Main Street, Edward Dickinson made Austin an offer that he couldn't afford to refuse. If his son agreed to stay in Amherst, Edward Dickinson would build him a new house on the land next door to the Homestead, using any plans that Austin and Susan chose. In addition, Edward Dickinson would take Austin into his law firm as a full partner.

Emily Dickinson was delighted. Not only would her brother remain close to his family, but when he married Susan Gilbert, Emily would also have her dearest friend living right next door.

By that time, most of Emily's girlhood friends had scattered, and the circle of boys and girls who had enjoyed such good times together was greatly diminished. Most of the young men had moved elsewhere after they graduated from Amherst. Many of the young women had married by the time they were in their mid-twenties. Abiah Root, to whom Emily wrote so often when she was at South Hadley Seminary, married a clergyman, as did Abby Wood. With her husband, Daniel Bliss, Abby went to Beirut, Lebanon, and helped him found a school that would later be known as American University.

Dickinson now had little in common with her former friends. Her refusal to join the church and her increasing withdrawal from the town's social activities had caused her to drift apart from those who remained. She needed a good friend, someone with whom she could talk about literature and perhaps share her own writing.

Susan Gilbert was such a person, and when Susan left Amherst to teach school in Baltimore, Emily Dickinson missed her sorely. She wrote many passionate letters to Susan, complaining about their separation. When Susan decided that teaching was not for her and returned to Amherst, Emily was overjoyed.

In the meantime, the Dickinsons were occupied with moving into the Homestead from the house on North Pleasant Street. Several improvements had been made to the house that Emily's grandfather built, including the addition of a water pump in the kitchen and a glass conservatory for Emily's flowers. The house next door was under construction, and Emily eagerly awaited the day when her brother and Susan would occupy it.

Austin Dickinson and Susan Gilbert married in Geneva, New York, on July 1, 1856, with none of the Dickinson family in attendance, and moved into the Evergreens soon after. Three hundred feet away lay the Homestead, the house into which Emily Dickinson moved in 1855 and rarely left thereafter. It was not long before a path was worn from the back door of the Homestead to the Evergreens.

The Evergreens' plan made it perfect for entertaining; in contrast, the Homestead seemed ideally suited for a writer seeking privacy. Emily Dickinson's bedroom, directly over the front parlor, had two windows. The south window overlooked the street and offered her a view of any visitor who might venture up the front walk, there or next door at the Evergreens. The west window offered a view of her brother's house, at least through the trees and other plantings in between.

Dickinson probably wrote the majority of her poems and many of her letters in this room, often late into the night by the dim light of candles or oil lamps. In the daytime, she often wrote downstairs at a table overlooking her garden. She must have also scribbled numerous other poems and letters at the kitchen table while waiting for bread to bake or a cake to cool.

With Susan Gilbert now living only a few hundred feet away, there was at first no need for her and Dickinson to continue their correspondence. Dickinson and Susan visited back and forth in person, and Dickinson was often present when Susan entertained. She called Austin and Susan "my crowd," and sometimes played the piano and sang for Susan's guests. One such evening, the story goes, Edward Dickinson came to fetch Emily home at midnight.

Many of Emily Dickinson's poems were written for or refer to Susan Gilbert Dickinson. In one of the earliest, the poet calls Susan her sister. In time, Emily Dickinson began writing to Susan almost daily. Of about 400 surviving notes and letters that she sent Susan over some 35 years, most were written after they became next-door neighbors.

These weren't ordinary letters recounting daily events, but usually brief and often intense exchanges of thought and ideas filled with personal and literary allusions. Both women were too involved with their own concerns and responsibilities to make long visits in person, although the path quickly worn between the houses was testimony of many visits back and forth by members of both households.

Susan Dickinson worked hard at planning and putting on gala dinner parties and the other gatherings for which she soon became known as the best local hostess. At the same time, Emily Norcross Dickinson's health had begun to decline to the extent that her daughters had to nurse her as well as attend to all the household duties.

Although Edward Dickinson had hired an Irish maid when they moved into the house, the Homestead required more work than one person could manage. With their father often absent with his various civic and professional duties, Austin Dickinson was an almost daily visitor, helping Lavinia and Emily with matters they couldn't handle themselves. In fact, Austin's sisters saw Austin almost as much after his marriage as they had when he was living at home.

As Emily Dickinson worked in secret honing her craft as a poet, she turned to her sister-in-law for advice. She sent Susan poems that Susan critiqued. For the criticism she had been given, Emily Dickinson was grateful, and she praised Susan's insight.

Although she had told no one else of her intentions, Emily Dickinson had by then made firm her decision to devote herself to her writing. An 1862 poem (657) details her choice of poetry over prose:

> I dwell in Possibility—
> A fairer House than Prose—
> More numerous of Windows—
> Superior—for Doors—
> ....
> Of Visitors—the fairest—
> For Occupation—This—
> The spreading wide my narrow Hands
> To gather Paradise—

In 1858, Austin Dickinson became acquainted with Samuel Bowles, the editor of the *Springfield Republican.* He and Mrs. Bowles became regular visitors to the Evergreens, where they met Emily Dickinson. As was her custom with people she liked, Dickinson began to correspond with Mr. Bowles. Her letters addressed him formally as "Mr. Bowles" or "Sir," while he called her "Queen Recluse."

From the 35 surviving letters and nearly 50 poems that she sent him (some addressed to his wife were obviously meant for Bowles), it seems that Dickinson felt much more connection with him than he did with her. Regardless of whether she fell hopelessly in love with Bowles, as has been speculated, at the least she probably hoped that he would understand her poetry and support her need to write it. Apparently he did neither, however, and although he continued their correspondence, he must also have made it clear that he did not share any hopes she might harbor about a romantic future with him.

In May 1861 Bowles anonymously published a Dickinson poem she had sent him. "The May Wine," as titled by Bowles, begins, "I taste a liquor never brewed...." In March 1862, before sailing to Europe, Bowles printed a poem that she had sent Susan. Without consulting its author, he edited "The Sleepers," as he titled "Safe in their Alabaster Chambers," to make its lines, punctuation, and capitalization look more like the other poetry of the day. Although it did not bear her name, Dickinson could not have been pleased to see her work so altered from the way she had written it.

Regardless of what Bowles thought of Dickinson as a woman or as a poet, she produced some of her most powerful love poems after they met. There are suggestions that the joy of first love is the inspiration for many of her poems written during this period. Perhaps Dickinson's most famous love poem (249) also dates from this period:

Wild Nights—Wild Nights!
Were I with thee
Wild Nights should be
Our luxury!

Futile—the Winds—
To a Heart in port—
Done with the Compass—
Done with the Chart!

Rowing in Eden—
Ah, the Sea!
Might I but moor—Tonight—
In Thee!

Later poems written during the same period speak of a terrible anguish the poet experiences as a result of being rejected, although she never specifically states in what way or by whom. One such memorable poem (280) begins "I felt a Funeral, in my Brain/And Mourners to and fro...." The last stanza goes on to suggest how greatly the experience of rejection affected the writer's mind:

And then a Plank in Reason, broke,
And I dropped down, and down—
And hit a World, at every plunge,
And Finished knowing—then—

In addition to the thwarted romance suggested by some of these poems, other problems weighed heavily upon Dickinson. Besides her concern over her mother's health, the poet also had her own spells of sickness, perhaps giving her even more reason to spend more time at home. Her tendency to catch cold easily served as a convenient excuse not to attend church, which she quit doing altogether by 1860.

Dickinson's close ties with Susan had begun to fray even before Susan gave birth to Edward (Ned) Dickinson in July of 1861. From then on, although Susan had adequate household help and continued to entertain lavishly, she often seemed to have little time to give to her sister-in-law. As a married woman with a child, Susan may have felt that she and Emily Dickinson had, at that point, little in common.

For whatever reasons, their estrangement was so complete that although Emily Dickinson continued to send notes across the hedge to the Evergreens, she did not set foot in her brother's house again for about 15 years.

An additional problem arose when it became clear that Austin and Susan Dickinson's marriage was becoming increasingly troubled. Susan had always had a mercurial temperament ("Sue fronts on the Gulf Stream," Dickinson once said), and Austin seems to have felt that his wife was more interested in the friends they entertained than she was in her own husband. Although Austin was doing well as a partner in his father's law practice, Susan's parties and dinners were financial drains on the family's finances.

For Austin, the Homestead offered a haven away from his wife and a noisy household that eventually grew to include his and Susan's three children as well as Susan's two orphaned nieces. When the strain on their brother began to show, Lavinia turned against Susan, whom she had once praised. In addition to Susan's treatment of her brother, Lavinia thought that Susan was also hurting her sister by neglecting Emily at a time when she badly needed a friend.

With Samuel Bowles no longer in the picture and having no one in Amherst she felt she could approach about her writing, Dickinson looked elsewhere for a mentor. She found what she sought in an unlikely place: the pages of the *Atlantic Monthly* magazine.

The Poet as a Riddle

In an essay titled "Advice to a Young Contributor" written for the April 1862 *Atlantic Monthly*, Thomas Wentworth Higginson decried the poor quality of writing that was being sent to its editors. Higginson seemed to Dickinson to be someone who recognized good writing when he saw it, a man with the ability to give an honest assessment of her poetry, if he was willing.

By this time, with hundred of poems already written and refined, Dickinson was hardly the sort of "young contributor" that Higginson had written about. She had developed some ability to be objective about her work and often revised a poem several times after its first writing, changing words that better suited her intentions.

She wrote on anything that came to hand; if plain paper was not available when the words of a poem came to her, she'd use the back of an envelope, a paper bag, or the reverse side of a letter she'd received. Later, after making a fair copy on a folded piece of paper, she usually destroyed the draft. She used all four sides of the sheet, and if a poem was longer than the paper, she attached another sheet with a pin. As her poems accumulated, she stacked four or five sheets together according to their themes or subject matter. Using cotton string, she sewed the left edges together and tied the ends in a bow. She kept these "fascicles" in a bureau drawer.

While Dickinson's gift for using words and the necessity to do so for her own peace of mind kept her writing, she wanted some assurance of the value of her work. In response to Higginson's *Atlantic Monthly* article, she sent him four poems, accompanied by a letter asking him to be her mentor.

Emily Dickinson seldom titled her poems, but the ones she enclosed have these first lines: "We play at Paste," "Safe in their Alabaster Chambers," "The nearest Dream recedes unrealized," and "I'll tell you how the Sun rose."

Apparently Higginson replied almost immediately. His letter has been lost, but her response indicates that he apparently asked questions about Dickinson's life. She responded with the same kind of enigmatic phrases she used in her poems.

Dickinson told Higginson that she could not judge her own work: "While my thought is undressed—I can make the distinction, but when I put them in the Gown—they look alike and numb."

She evaded his question about her age and added that she had "made no verse—but one or two—until this winter," an obvious untruth.

Higginson probably asked Dickinson why she wrote, to which she replied: "I had a terror—since September—I could tell to none—and so I sing, as the Boy does by the Burying Ground—because I am afraid—"

She never explained the nature of the "terror," although many believe it was the dashing of her hope that Samuel Bowles would be her mentor, or more. This possibility is reinforced by a later comment in the same letter: "... my Tutor, died—and for several years, my Lexicon—was my only companion—Then I found one more—but he was not contented I be his scholar—so he left the Land."

Dickinson had depended upon Newton, who died, and then on Samuel Bowles, who had already declined to be what Dickinson wanted by the time he went to England for several months in 1862.

Her letter continued to address Higginson's questions. Then Dickinson appealed for Higginson's help: "I would like to learn—Could you tell me how to grow—or is it unconveyed—like Melody or Witchcraft?"

Dickinson probably intended the poems she sent Higginson to represent a cross section of her work. The selections show her interest in nature, as well as the major themes of immortality and the search for religious certainty that are present in so many of her poems. Despite the craftsmanship apparent in her use of metaphor and personification, Dickinson's poetry was quite different from what was then being published. Even though Higginson was intrigued, he found it difficult to understand either the poems or their author.

Why would anyone who could make such powerful images deliberately ignore the use of conventional rhyme and meter to present them more "normally"? Higginson praised what he could but advised her to "delay publication," no doubt in the belief that Dickinson's poetry, in its present state, would never find an audience.

Dickinson assured Higginson that she did not wish to publish. She also thanked him for his "surgery" on her poems and gave a reason for writing that is similar to that mentioned in her previous reply: "I felt a palsy, here—the Verses just relieve."

Writing was more a passion than a pastime for Emily Dickinson. A necessary part of her life, it was Dickinson's way of expressing her emotional reaction to the world. Finally, she asked Higginson to be her "Preceptor." He apparently agreed and invited her to come to Boston, where he wanted to introduce her to the leading literary lights of the day. She refused, instead inviting him to come to Amherst. He did—eight years later.

In the meantime, they continued to exchange letters. When Higginson confessed that some of her lines were "beyond his knowledge," she expressed surprise. Dickinson's puzzlement that Higginson claimed not to understand her might have been because two of the poems she sent are not only among her most conventional but also those that she thought should have particular appeal for Higginson.

Higginson had been appointed a lieutenant colonel in the 29th Regiment, in which he served in South Carolina during the Civil War. Higginson was also a "radical" Unitarian minister, pastor of the Free Church of Worcester, Massachusetts. Dickinson must have believed he would appreciate the religious thought expressed in one of her most conventional verses (324), written several years before:

> Some keep the Sabbath going to Church—
> I keep it, staying at Home—
> With a Bobolink for a Chorister—
> And an Orchard, for a Dome—
>
> Some keep the Sabbath in Surplice—
> I just wear my Wings—
> And instead of tolling the Bell, for Church,
> Our little Sexton—sings.
>
> God preaches, a noted Clergyman—
> And the sermon is never long,
> So instead of getting to Heaven, at last—
> I'm going, all along.

There is little question that Dickinson valued Higginson's friendship, yet she could not apply his advice to her poetry.

After that letter, written in the summer of 1862, there was a gap in their correspondence. It resumed in February of the next year, when Higginson was in South Carolina as the commander of a black regiment. Dickinson continued to send him more poems, but not for his criticism.

At the time Dickinson was dealing with her own personal crises, the entire country was immersed in the trauma of the Civil War. When news of the war began to reach Amherst College in April of 1861, it was all the college's president and administration could do to keep all the students from rushing off immediately in response to President Lincoln's call for volunteers. Commencement was held a month early, without the usual Dickinson reception. The Dickinson family had not taken part in the many reform movements that swept New England in the decade before the Civil War, including the cause of abolition. Unlike her contemporary, Harriet Beecher Stowe, Emily Dickinson never took up her pen in protest of slavery.

The Dickinsons had no immediate family members participating in the fighting. When Austin Dickinson was about to be drafted into military service, he paid $500 for a substitute to go in his place. Still, the war was a constant worry that could not be ignored, and it added to Emily Dickinson's personal unhappiness.

When Frazar Stearns, the young son of the Amherst College president, was killed in action, Dickinson joined the whole town in mourning over the war that had so cruelly extinguished the boy's bright promise. In a letter to her Norcross cousins, she wrote, "Sorrow seems more general than it did, and not the estate of a few persons, since the war began."

Dickinson carried on an extensive personal correspondence with family members, lifelong friends, and many other people, such as Higginson. Letter writing was considered an art in those days, with much care taken with letters to friends. Among the pages and pages of writing discovered after Dickinson's death are rough drafts of many of her letters, including some that she apparently never finished or sent.

From her first known letters to a friend when she was eleven to notes written only a few days before her death, Dickinson produced an amazingly large volume of correspondence. Most of her letters contain 1,500 to 3,000 words, written in a lively, direct style that entertains as much as it informs. Dickinson kept no daily diary of her activities, and few of her letters are dated. However, they show what interested her at the time, and because of the changes in her handwriting over the years, scholars have been able to arrange most of them chronologically.

In addition to her letters, Dickinson wrote short notes to accompany the gifts of flowers or food she sent to ill or bereaved neighbors or as thanks for things done for her or her family. Many of Dickinson's letters have been described as "prose poems" because parts are written in the same meter and employ the same kind of quick wit and epigrams she uses in her stand-alone verses.

Some of the letters are almost painfully personal. The controversial "Master" letters, whose intended recipient is still unknown, may or may not have been actually sent. But Dickinson did send—and receive—other love letters.

Taken together, Dickinson's correspondence makes interesting reading. Like her poems, the letters sometimes conceal as much as they reveal, but they provide a fascinating glimpse of Dickinson's life and her work as a poet.

Even while carrying on a voluminous correspondence, Dickinson did not neglect her poetry. In 1862, the year of Frazar Stearns' death and her appeal to Higginson to be her "Preceptor," Dickinson wrote about 366 poems, including many considered among her finest. The time of her greatest emotional turmoil also marked the peak of her creativity.

Dickinson wrote, at least in part, to forestall her "Terror" and to ease the pain of her feelings of rejection, but she also continued to look at the world around her for her subject matter. Although her serious poetry usually receives the most attention, Dickinson's interest in "riddles" led her to produce many interesting verses.

Dickinson's poems rarely refer to current events, but one among the many that she wrote some time around 1862 is a riddle poem (585) that seems directly related to her father's work in bringing "progress" to Amherst a few years earlier:

> I like to hear it lap the Miles—
> And lick the Valleys up—
> And stop to feed itself at Tanks—
> And then—prodigious step
>
> Around a Pile of Mountains—
> And supercilious peer
> In Shanties—by the sides of Roads—
> And then a Quarry pare....

Although Dickinson does not say so directly, "It" is, of course, a railroad train. It is also an exception to the other riddle poems, which deal with the natural, rather than the synthetic, as in this poem (1114):

The largest fire ever known
Occurs each Afternoon—
Discovered is without surprise
Proceeds without concern—
Consumes and no report to men
An Occidental Town,
Rebuilt another morning
To be burned down again.

One of Dickinson's most famous poems speaks of "A narrow Fellow in the Grass" (986). Published without her permission as "The Snake," its title spoiled the riddle. The poet describes another of Nature's creatures (1034):

His Bill an Auger is
His Head, a Cap and Frill
He laboreth at every Tree
A Worm, His utmost Goal—

Poems like these and "I'll tell you how the sun rose—/A ribbon at a time—" (318), which she sent to Higginson, reveal Dickinson's ability to closely observe and analyze Nature and then to record her impressions in concise, yet strikingly original words. The poems may appear to be composed in haste, but the finished product is often the result of many drafts.

By the time she had reached her mid-thirties, Emily Dickinson's life had apparently settled into a routine. With a very few exceptions, she rarely left the Homestead and neither visited others nor received visitors herself. She continued to write poetry, but not in the torrents produced in 1862. She wrote 141 poems in 1863 and 174 in 1864. After that, she averaged 50 poems yearly.

Dickinson began to wear white dresses, fitted by a dressmaker to her sister Lavinia, and was well on the way to earning her reputation for being "odd."

However, life had not finished dealing with Emily Dickinson. She had many other poems and letters to write. Some of her greatest sorrows still lay ahead.

Yet, she would also experience unexpected joy.

My Business is Circumference

Dickinson's habit of writing long into the night by poor light may have damaged her vision. Early in 1864 she consulted a Boston ophthalmologist, who recommended a course of treatment that took seven months. During that time she lived with her orphaned Norcross cousins, Fanny and Louisa, then 16 and 22 years old, in a boarding house in Cambridgeport, Massachusetts. Being away from her familiar, beloved Homestead would have been bad enough, but Dickinson was also forbidden to use her eyes for reading and writing, the twin occupations that meant the most to her. Her young cousins did all they could to make her comfortable, but on her return home, Dickinson wrote another cousin that she had been "in Siberia."

Back in Amherst, Dickinson resumed her share of the housework and plunged into reading the works of Shakespeare, her favorite author. ("Why is any other book needed?" she once asked rhetorically.) She also continued to write letters and added to the growing store of poems in her bureau drawer. Writing was as necessary to her as breathing, and her poetry was not just what she wrote: it was who she was.

In one of her early letters to Higginson, Dickinson declared, "My business is circumference." Her use of the last word has more than one meaning. "Circumference" limits, but it also encompasses. Dickinson intended to encompass the truth of life and human experience and then capture those telling moments and recreate them through her poems. It was a large order, indeed. As biographer Richard Sewall puts it, "She set out to be Expositor, Interpreter, Analyst, Orpheus—all in one."

Many poets besides Dickinson have sought to express the ineffable, to make clear matters too overwhelming for ordinary words. If she didn't always succeed in relating the truths that she sought, it wasn't for lack of trying.

Dickinson sought those rare moments when the barrier that separates the ordinary world from the sublime drops away. The overwhelming awe connected with these transcendent moments had an element of fear or terror, especially when the poet contemplated the great mysteries of death and immortality.

The words Dickinson uses to express her feelings are chosen with care and economy. They are often so embedded in metaphors and other figurative language as to be literally "untranslatable." In other words, like an idiom from a foreign language, many of Dickinson's phrases cannot be restated in ordinary speech, even though the reader understands their meaning. This "untranslatable" quality pervades even poems about mundane subjects, not just those in which the poet contemplates the meaning and scope of life and death.

For example, when describing an encounter with a common garden snake, Dickinson could say that she felt afraid or that the experience gave her "chill bumps." Anyone would understand those words, which accurately assess such a situation.

However, Dickinson takes the reader to a much deeper level. Of the "narrow Fellow in the grass" (986), she concludes:

> But never met this Fellow
> Attended, or alone
> Without a tighter breathing
> And Zero at the Bone—

Rapid ("tighter") breathing is a literal physiological result of fear, but "zero at the bone," a medical impossibility, almost takes the reader's own breath away.

Dickinson achieved such effects in poem after poem, sometimes twisting the meaning of ordinary words and adding surprise endings. At times, the poems don't seem to end as much as to trail off into silence, as if the poet has said all she can in words.

Dickinson called her "Lexicon" her only companion after she lost her first tutor. Interestingly, Noah Webster, the compiler of both the speller that Dickinson would have used in school and the first dictionary of American English words, was the Dickinsons' neighbor. Webster's granddaughter, Emily Fowler, was one of Emily Dickinson's girlhood friends. The first edition of Webster's dictionary was published in 1828; Dickinson probably used the second edition, published in 1856, which contained 70,000 words. She constantly thumbed through its pages in search of words with the precise meanings she sought for her poems.

From the newspapers and magazines of the day, Dickinson also gathered words related to current exploration and geography. In a poem (511) that begins "If you were coming in the Fall—" Dickinson speaks of "Van Dieman's land," the name for what is now Tasmania. She also knew about the exploration of Australia; in a letter to Higginson, Dickinson called herself "the only Kangaroo among the Beauty."

Dickinson took care in the way she placed her chosen words on paper. She capitalized most nouns, in the German manner. That and her unique punctuation, in which the dash rules supreme, are far from conventional. Through the years, many editors have tried to "correct" what they consider to be the poet's "errors," only to weaken and change her poems for the worse.

Dickinson's poems look quite different as she wrote them in their bundled fascicles than they do in print. The dashes are not all straight, nor are they all the same length. In ordinary use, a dash indicates a sudden change in thought. Dashes also slow down the reader, providing more time to get the full weight of each line. A dash makes an indefinite ending to a line. Sometimes she uses dashes as a substitute for a colon to introduce lists or series of items. Dickinson might also have intended her dashes to be a sort of musical notation as to whether the end of a line should have a rising inflection, as in a question, or a falling inflection, as in a statement.

Most of Dickinson's meters come directly from the hymns that she learned as a child, adaptations of psalms that had been set to music by the Englishman Isaac Watts a hundred years earlier. Number 100 in the hymnal used by generations of New Englanders, the "Doxology" (its tune is still known as "Old Hundred"), is an example of one of Dickinson's basic rhythmic forms:

Praise God, from Whom all blessings flow;
Praise Him, all creatures here below;
Praise Him above, ye heav'nly host;
Praise Father, Son and Holy Ghost.

Most of the leading poets writing in the English language during Dickinson's time, including Dickinson's favorites, the Brownings, preferred graceful lines of iambic pentameter, which has five accented syllables to each line. In a time when poetic language was generally "high-flown" and poets used difficult and complex verse forms such as the sonnet, Dickinson's four-line stanzas seem almost crude by comparison.

Her most widely used form is "common meter," in which lines of eight iambic syllables alternate with lines of six iambic syllables. These can be divided into four and three accented syllables, as in the traditional ballad form. Unlike the ballad, common meter lines rhyme in the pattern *abab* rather than *abcb*.

Because of their metrical similarity, the words of Dickinson's common meter poem that begins "Because I could not stop for Death—" (712) can be sung to the tune of "Amazing Grace."

However, Dickinson's poetry cannot always be bound to a predictable pattern. One line may have an extra syllable or two, and another may have fewer. She uses many "slant" rhymes, as in line-ending words such as "June" and "join;" and enjambment, in which a line doesn't neatly end a thought.

Dickinson's later poetry is highly condensed. Omitting some words, she attaches multiple meanings to others, as in this brief poem (89):

Some things that fly there be—Birds—Hours—the Bumblebee—
Of these no Elegy.

> Some things that stay there be—
> Grief—Hills—Eternity—
> Nor this behooveth me.
>
> There are that resting, rise.
> Can I expound the skies?
> How still the Riddle lies!

This "riddle poem" contains several condensed thoughts. In the first stanza, things that "fly" are birds, hours, and bees. Birds and bees literally fly, whereas the "flight" of time is figurative. The stanza's conclusion states that no one mourns the flight of birds, bees, or time, and hence they need no "Elegy."

In the second stanza, the poet mentions things that "stay" or remain, including the emotion of grief, perhaps brought on by the losses of time; literal "Hills;" and the most enduring of all, "Eternity." She accepts that all three of these are always present, but that does not concern ("behoove") her.

The third stanza begins with another elliptical statement. "There are [those] that resting, [in their graves] rise [in the Resurrection]." Then the poet asks a rhetorical question that shows that this is a mystery, a riddle she cannot "expound" or comprehend. Only God can reconcile time (implied in the first stanza) and "Eternity" so that human beings, bound by the limitations of time and mortality, can find fulfillment in eternity. Only God, Dickinson concludes, can understand and bring about the resurrection of the dead.

"Still" in the final stanza conveys the double meaning of the absence or motion and a continuation of action. The poem's final word, "lies," can be taken to mean rests, or, to one who lacks faith, the resurrection is a "lie," a falsehood.

The division of the poem into three stanzas of three lines each, with three feet per line, serves to reinforce the Trinity as being the agent of human redemption on earth.

On the surface, Dickinson lived the quiet life of a reclusive "maiden lady" as she continued writing poems she had no intention to publish. However, her inner life continued to be far richer and fuller than anyone suspected.

In August of 1870, Higginson finally paid a visit to the woman who had, over a period of eight years, sent him about 100 of her poems. Writing about the meeting later, Higginson described Dickinson as a small, plain woman who spoke in a soft, breathless, and childlike voice. Despite telling Higginson that she never saw strangers and hardly knew what to say, she apparently talked most of the time he was there. As was the case with her letters, Higginson didn't understand much of Dickinson's conversation, but he sensed her pleasure in having someone with whom she could talk about poetry. Although he hadn't succeeded in his attempt to lead her poetry into more traditional channels, he acknowledged her talent. Back home, he told his wife that he had never met anyone who "drained his nerve power" so much as Emily Dickinson.

Three years later, Higginson returned to Amherst for a lecture and paid Dickinson a final visit, more as her friend than her teacher. They continued to correspond off and on for a few more years, but Higginson was no longer her lifeline to the world of literature.

In 1872 Edward Dickinson resigned his position as treasurer of Amherst College. The post was assumed by Austin Dickinson, who had made his mark on Amherst civic affairs in much the same way as his father had, being moderator of the town meeting and serving important posts in the church. By then Austin and Susan had two children, although their marriage continued to be strained.

On June 16, 1874, Edward Dickinson was in court in Boston when he collapsed and died. Emily Dickinson was both devastated and somewhat surprised at the depth of her grief for the father who had often seemed so stern and distant. She could not bring herself to attend his funeral and withdrew even further into herself and her home.

A year to the day after Edward Dickinson's death, his widow suffered a paralytic stroke that left her bedridden. For the next seven years, Emily and Lavinia Dickinson shared the constant burden of their mother's care. Emily Dickinson still wrote many letters but produced fewer poems.

During these troubled times, Higginson showed some of Dickinson's poems to Helen Hunt, whom Emily Dickinson had known at the Amherst Academy as Helen Fiske. She had married a man named Hunt and been widowed during the Civil War. An acclaimed poet herself, Helen began to correspond with her old friend. In 1875 she married again, becoming Helen Hunt Jackson.

Jackson found Dickinson's poems remarkable and urged her to publish them. With or without Dickinson's permission, Jackson included "Success Is Counted Sweetest" (67), one of the first poems Dickinson had sent Higginson, in her anthology, *A Masque of Poets*. Jackson didn't use Dickinson's name, and many thought that the author was Ralph Waldo Emerson.

Jackson proved to be a good friend and one of the few persons outside her family circle whom Dickinson allowed to visit her. Jackson asked permission to be Dickinson's literary executor, but before any agreement could be reached, Jackson died.

Another caller that Dickinson always welcomed was Judge Otis Phillips Lord, appointed Chief Justice of the Massachusetts Supreme Court in 1875. An Amherst graduate and Edward Dickinson's close personal and political friend, Lord had attended the yearly commencement receptions for years. In the early 1870s, Judge and Mrs. Lord continued their frequent visits to the Homestead even after Edward Dickinson's death.

Dickinson's letters in 1878, a year after Judge Lord's wife died, make it clear that at some point, the long friendship between her and the judge had grown into a deep, passionate love. This time, the object of Dickinson's affection returned her love in full measure, and several of her poems reflect her joy.

Emily Dickinson was 47 and Lord was 65, but the difference in their ages did not affect the relationship. Although the Judge lived too far away to visit Amherst often, he and Dickinson exchanged weekly letters, and he came to see her when he could. No proof exists on either side, but it is doubtful that Judge Lord ever asked Dickinson to marry him.

At one time Dickinson would have considered leaving her home as a bride—several poems have that theme—but those days were long past. She was tied to her home and committed to the care of her mother. Even had Dickinson been willing, Judge Lord's family was firmly against his marrying again. Until Lord's death in March 1884, the couple seems to have enjoyed a measure of much-needed happiness.

Emily Dickinson also took pleasure in Austin and Susan's offspring. Together with the neighboring children of Reverend Jenkins, her niece and nephews often played around the Homestead. One story says that Dickinson sometimes lowered them a basket of baked treats from her upstairs window.

Gilbert (Gib), the youngest of her brother and Susan's children, was Dickinson's favorite. A bright child with a sunny disposition, Gib was welcome to visit the Homestead whenever he liked. When he left behind a coat or a book, his Aunt Emily saw that it was returned to the Evergreens, along with a little poem, a flower, or a treat.

On November 14, 1882, Emily Norcross Dickinson died, and once again Emily Dickinson mourned the loss of a parent. As she put it, "... the dear Mother that could not walk, has *flown*."

Less than a year later, eight-year-old Gilbert Dickinson became ill with typhoid fever. For the first time in fifteen years, Emily Dickinson walked the path to the Evergreens, to stand watch over his sickbed. When he died on October 5, 1883, the Homestead and the Evergreens were plunged into deep mourning.

For neither household would life ever again be the same.

The War Between the Houses

Gilbert's death shattered Emily Dickinson as not even the deaths of her parents had done. The day after he died, she took to her bed with a "nervous exhaustion" from which she was slow to recover.

Had Gilbert Dickinson lived, he might have brought about reconciliation between the households of the Homestead and the

Evergreens, both of whose residents adored him. In their mutual grief, Susan and Emily Dickinson might have renewed their friendship. But the notes Dickinson sent to Susan concern the mystery of the loss of such a beautiful child, rather than reach out in sympathy to his grieving mother.

Their son's death might have brought his parents to comfort and discover new affection for each other. Instead, it had the opposite effect. Totally absorbed in her own grief, Susan turned away from her husband, who turned to the other woman in his life.

Austin Dickinson first met 24-year-old Mabel Loomis Todd when her husband came to Amherst College as professor of astronomy in 1881. They became frequent visitors to the Evergreens, and when Emily Dickinson heard that Todd was a talented musician, she invited her to come to the Homestead to play and sing for her. As was her custom when callers came, Emily Dickinson stayed in the hallway and listened, but she did not meet her guest. Instead, she sent her a note of thanks, together with a poem and a flower.

Todd's record of her impressions of Dickinson's behavior helped create the image of "the myth of Amherst,"—the strange, white-clad woman recluse who wrote odd poems. Later, an entry in Todd's diary notes that Susan Dickinson had read her some "powerful" poems written by her sister-in-law.

Although Todd visited the Homestead many more times, she never saw Emily Dickinson face-to-face. However, because Austin Dickinson spent a great deal of time there, in part to get away from his unhappy home, Todd soon got to know him quite well.

Their detailed diaries tell of the growing attraction between Austin Dickinson and Todd, which in September 1882 led to the start of a love affair that scandalized Amherst and lasted until Austin's death in 1895.

What Emily Dickinson thought of her brother's affair can only be supposed. She must have known about it, because Austin and Mabel often met privately at the Homestead. She might have thought he deserved the happiness that he had failed to find with his wife, particularly after the way Susan turned from him after their son's death. Legally, Austin had inherited the Homestead from his father and could render his sisters homeless if he chose. The fact that he had financed their household for many years could make it difficult for Lavinia and Emily to criticize Austin. However, he was devoted to his sisters, and they were always loyal to him.

In 1884, the same year Judge Lord died, Dickinson's health began to decline. Her condition worsened at the beginning of January of 1886, and in early May, she sent her last and shortest letter to her Norcross cousins. It read, "Little Cousins, Called back. Emily."

Dickinson died of Bright's disease just before six o'clock on the evening of May 15, 1886.

Although she and her sister-in-law had not been close, as they once were, for many years, Susan Dickinson came from the Evergreens to wash and dress Emily Dickinson's body for burial. She also wrote an eloquent obituary that appeared in the *Springfield Republican* newspaper. After praising Emily Dickinson's good works and saying, "Her talk and writings were like no one's else," Susan Dickinson concluded with these words:

> To her life was rich, and all aglow with God and immortality. With no creed, no formalized faith, hardly knowing the names of dogmas, she walked this life with the gentleness and reverence of old saints, with the firm step of martyrs who sing while they suffer. How better to note the flight of this "soul of fire in a shell of pearl" than by her own words?
>
> Morns like these, we parted;
> Noons like these, she rose;
> Fluttering first, then firmer,
> To her fair repose.

The funeral was simple. She had not wanted a church funeral service, and so a small group of mourners gathered at the Homestead. Scripture was read, and the Rev. Jenkins, whose children had played around Homestead, led in prayer. Higginson read "Immortality," by Emily Brontë, a favorite poem that Dickinson had read to Lavinia. Emily Dickinson's coffin was then carried out the back door of the Homestead and across three fields to the cemetery, where she was laid to rest beside her parents. Susan's obituary had said Dickinson's home "proved the fit atmosphere for her worth and work," but no one was aware of just how much "work" Dickinson had produced until, a few days after her sister's death, Lavinia Dickinson found the astonishing store of poems. Lavinia knew that her sister's work deserved publication, but she had no idea how to go about the massive task involved in getting the hundreds of bundled poems ready to be printed.

By this time, Mabel Loomis Todd had published several short stories. She had a typing machine, clumsy though it was, and she genuinely admired Emily Dickinson's poetry. Lavinia asked her help, and in 1887 Todd started to work on copying the bundled fascicles.

In 1889, Todd enlisted the aid of Higginson. She needed his literary skills to help edit the poems and his reputation to open publishers' doors. Together, they edited (and sometimes rewrote) enough poems to fill three volumes. The poems were given titles, and the original punctuation, rhyme, word choices, and meter were altered to make the poems more traditional, just as Higginson had wanted from the start.

After several other publishers declined to take the poems, Thomas Niles, editor of Roberts Brothers of Boston, agreed to produce a small edition of 116 poems, provided that Lavinia Dickinson paid for the plates. The first printing in 1890 quickly sold out, and Todd and Higginson produced a further volume of poems in 1891. Todd also collected and edited Dickinson's letters, in two volumes, in 1894. In 1896, without Higginson (who was then 71 and in ill health), Todd published a third volume of Dickinson's poems. When Austin Dickinson died in 1895, Todd put on mourning clothes, although both her husband and Austin's wife were still living. Soon after, the tensions between the Dickinsons and the Todds culminated in a lawsuit over land that Mabel Loomis Todd claimed Austin had promised her as payment for her work in editing his sister's poetry. Todd alleged that Lavinia Dickinson had signed a paper agreeing to the transfer, and then changed her mind. Lavinia denied knowing that the paper she had signed was a deed, and the matter went to trial in 1898. Lavinia Dickinson won the lawsuit, but Todd left town with over 600 of Emily Dickinson's poems that were still in her possession. When Lavinia died in 1899, her portion went to Susan Dickinson. Susan died in 1913, and a year later, Susan's daughter, Martha Dickinson Bianchi, published poems Emily Dickinson had sent to Susan and her family in *The Single Hound*, followed by further new editions and books of collected poems in 1924, 1929, 1930, 1935, and 1937.

Then in 1945, Todd and her daughter, Millicent Todd Bingham, produced another book of "new poems." Finally that same year, Thomas H. Johnson published an edition that contains all of Dickinson's poems, presented as much as possible as originally written. Including some poems that are edited or rewritten, this edition contains about two thousand entries. It is likely that all Dickinson poems have at last been discovered. However, some dusty old New England attic could yet yield previously unknown material, including some of the thousands of missing notes and letters to and from Dickinson. However, they would probably not shed much more light on the enigmatic, reclusive genius of Emily Dickinson.

Louis Untermeyer, who included the nineteenth century poets Emily Dickinson and Walt Whitman in his 1950 edition of *Modern American Poetry*, said that "paradox was her native element" and then added an evaluation that will probably stand the test of time: "She who contained a universe did not need the world."

The Homestead, where Emily Dickinson lived all but fifteen years of her life, is open to the public for tours from March to mid-December. The poet's books and writing desk and the bureau where her poems were found are on view, and the grounds are planted in the kinds of flowers that Dickinson cultivated.

Special events take place around December 10 in honor of the poet's birthday. In December 1999, a replica of a white gown that Dickinson was known to have worn arrived at the Homestead in time to be displayed as part of the birthday celebration. The original white dress dates from about 1878-1882 and is made of cotton fabric with mother-of-pearl buttons. It was not a particularly unusual or expensive garment for its time. After Dickinson's death, her sister gave the dress to a cousin. In 1946, the recipient's sister gave the dress to the Amherst Historical Society. For many years it was displayed at the Homestead. Because of the dress's age and the stress of being exposed to light and being hung on a mannequin, it was decided a replica should be made and the original placed in archival storage. No one knows how much the original dress cost, but the bill for the two replicas came to $10,000.

Next door to the Homestead, the Evergreens, where Martha Dickinson Bianchi lived until her death in 1943, is being restored and will also be open to the public.

Emily Dickinson's grave is in the West Cemetery on Triangle Street. Her original tombstone bore only her initials, but the words "Called Back" were added later by Martha Dickinson Bianchi.

Other sites of interest in Amherst include the Jones Library and Frost Library at Amherst College, both of which have manuscripts and special collections of Emily Dickinson and Robert Frost, a modern poet with Amherst connections.

SANDRA McCHESNEY

A View from the Window: The Poetry of Emily Dickinson

"I see New Englandly," said Emily Dickinson in a poem (285) written about 1861.[1]

At the time Dickinson had no way of knowing that her way of seeing would become a beacon for scholars all over the globe. Increasing numbers of people try to see her world through her eyes, searching her poems and correspondence for minute clues to enlighten their understanding of one of the most remarkable minds and prolific writing careers in American literature. In her more than 1,700 poems, Dickinson did "see New Englandly," combining her "Puritan heritage and the Yankee background," reproducing "as far as is possible in verse the qualities of New England speech, laconic brevity, directness, cadence."[2] What she saw, however, she then filtered through her own processes of perception and contemplation, her New England background providing the tools for thinking and her method of thinking providing an outlook that forged far beyond conventional mores.[3]

Background: Family History and Early Years

Emily Dickinson, born on December 10, 1830, in Amherst, Massachusetts, lived a life of privilege as the elder daughter of a prominent family in a small New England town. Her grandfather, Samuel Fowler Dickinson, helped to found Amherst Academy and then Amherst College and served several terms as a state legislator. A staunch Calvinist, he sank his personal funds into these two religious-based educational institutions because he was so deeply committed to upholding moral character as he envisioned it and to spreading the gospel. Attorney Edward Dickinson, Samuel's son and Emily's father, followed Samuel's lead, serving in many capacities in his community: treasurer of Amherst College, member of the Massachusetts legislature, and representative to the Thirty-third Congress in Washington, D.C. Although his duties took him from home, Edward Dickinson remained thoroughly aware of and in control of the activities of his family, as was the custom of his time and position. Emily's mother, Emily Norcross Dickinson, a quiet, self-effacing woman, devoted herself to keeping a serene household for her husband, again as was the custom of the community. Emily and her younger sister, Lavinia, neither of whom married, assisted Mrs. Dickinson, equally dutiful and constant in their labors in the house and garden. Their brother, Austin, continued the family's dedication to Amherst College, serving as treasurer while he practiced the legal profession, making his marital home adjacent to his parents'. Although Emily graduated from Amherst Academy, attended South Hadley Seminary for nearly a year, and was extremely well read, her daily life as a young woman revolved completely around her home and family. Because of her family's status, Emily helped entertain a number of eminent guests and frequent visitors. A witty, popular teenager, she displayed in her private letters a poise and command of language based on an extensive knowledge of the Bible, Shakespeare, the classics, and male and female writers of the period, such as Ralph Waldo Emerson; Charlotte, Emily, and Anne Brontë; Charles Dickens; and George Eliot. However, unlike the other members of her family, Emily gradually withdrew from outward involvement in the community during her twenties, eventually becoming the most famous recluse in American literature. Her journey into herself, expressed in her poetry, created a record of the unfolding of a unique literary style that continues to fascinate scholars around the world.

Awakening of the Poet

Dickinson did exhibit signs as she was growing up of the introspective poet she would become. Her artistic character showed primarily in sensitive reaction to people, situations, and surroundings. This "acute sensitivity," says Thomas H. Johnson, "was a handicap that she bore as one who lives with a disability." (L)[4] She shared her feelings extensively and often in letters to family members and selected friends. In a letter to Abiah Root on September 8, 1846, she wrote, "How swiftly summer has fled & what report has it borne to heaven of misspent time & wasted hours? The ceaseless flight of the seasons is to me a very solemn thought, & yet Why do we not strive to make a better improvement of them?"[5] Dickinson was fifteen years old at the time. At that age, then as now, most young girls were concerned with clothes and hair and social activities; Dickinson was already measuring her days with the weights and balances of a philosopher.

To the recipients of her letters, Dickinson conveyed the urgent need of an immediate reply or visit. Her language was often disconsolate, a convention of the times, but she managed to couch her feelings in prose that sounded like poetry. Beginning a letter to her cousin, Emily Fowler Ford, probably early in 1850, Dickinson started with only an underline as a salutation, no name attached. "That isn't an *empty* blank where I began—," she explains, "it is so full of affection that you cant see any—that's all."[6] Filling empty blanks with information only she could see became a device that Dickinson fine-tuned; sometimes she explained the meanings to her readers, sometimes she left them guessing her purport. The following year, on September 23, Emily writes to Austin, giving an example of her incipient ear for rhythm as her liveliness and sense of humor spill out in a burst of glee: "I could fancy that skeleton cats ever caught spectre rats in dim old nooks and corners."[7] Combined with her introspection, her inscrutability, her humor, and her sense of language, she also reveled in a love of nature that was a foundation of her family's daily life. Whereas Edward and Austin Dickinson occupied themselves with prodigious public plantings of trees, Emily immersed herself in discovering and describing the miniature world of a leaf, a blade of grass, or an insect: "The Bee is not afraid of me./I know the Butterfly./The pretty people in the Woods/Receive me cordially—."[8] Placing herself directly into the landscape, she then began to relate the tiny to the infinite as she explored in poetry the relationships of the natural world at hand with the boundless world of the universe.

Because Dickinson spent her days in the unending round of household tasks necessary to survival and comfort, her opportunities for writing the poetry that began to teem in her brain were often lost among the moments and hours of what she sometimes expressed as drudgery. In that era, women were responsible not only for sewing, mending, cooking, and baking but also for such time-consuming tasks as candle-making and preserving all of the produce of home gardens and orchards. In addition, spring cleaning, a New England obsession, meant not only thorough dusting and scrubbing of walls, windows, and furniture but also taking up heavy wall-to-wall carpeting and beating it clean outdoors. Millicent Todd Bingham, in her detailed depiction of Dickinson's home and family, describes Dickinson's feelings: "For that particular activity Emily had succinct words: 'House' is being 'cleaned.' I prefer pestilence."[9] Dickinson's particular contribution to daily meals was baking and making desserts, but there were occasions when she had to spend more unwelcome time in the kitchen. Unable to avoid cooking regular meals during one of her mother's illnesses, Dickinson shared her woes with Abiah Root in early May, 1850: "Father and Austin still clamor for food, and I, like a martyr am feeding them. Wouldn't you love to see me in these bonds of great despair?"[10] Dickinson struggled with her unorthodox resistance to the domesticity that she had been reared from infancy to accept as woman's given duty. Although she could not totally escape her domestic responsibilities, she nevertheless in her twenties began to retreat to her room as often as possible, as she felt the ever-increasing need to express in writing the tumultuous growth of intellect burgeoning within her. Accepting and respecting her own reasoning, she simply could not renounce the need to pay attention to her own thoughts, which compelled her to find the opportunities to record those musings. "If she was ever to 'flee to her mind,'" said Millicent Todd Bingham, "time must be snatched from some chore waiting to be finished. A chance to be alone with her books and her thoughts was her reward, frequently long delayed."[11] Dickinson's writing, indulged at every possible moment, was nonetheless virtually unknown to her family, even though they lived in each other's constant company. Her sister Lavinia did remark upon Emily's quiet demeanor as the family gathered in the kitchen on long, cold New England winter evenings. Mr. Dickinson read "lonely and rigorous" books; Mrs. Dickinson mended or darned stockings; Austin studied; Lavinia read the newspaper. Emily sat quietly. Lavinia explained: Emily "'had to think. She was the only one of us who had that to do.'"[12] Although her thinking may have been noticed, her writing was not. "As her letters indicate," continued Bingham, "she often wrote in her room late at night while the others slept .... No one, no one to the very end, ever dreamed of the magnitude of the task to which her 'real' life had been devoted."[13] Her own family was never aware of the extent of her writings, small parts of which she began to share with a select few family members and friends. Even her father, who built his life around words and often praised his son Austin's cleverness in writing, never knew of his daughter's literary genius.

Themes and Symbols: Dickinson as Visionary

Dickinson wrote poetry for nearly thirty years. In that span of time, she created approximately 2,000 poems, fewer than a dozen of which were published in her lifetime. Therefore, she had little feedback from either an appreciative or an uncomplimentary audience. Also, Dickinson asked for criticism from very few persons and sometimes declined to heed their advice. Thus, her most constant confidant, inspiration, and critic was herself. As subject, she provided an array of dichotomies: strength/fragility; boldness/timidity; certainty/questioning; health/frailty; Christian/pagan. As an analyst, she explored her psyche untiringly, reaching conclusions and expressing those intellectual leaps in her poetry. In his psychoanalytical work *After Great Pain: The Inner Life of Emily Dickinson*, John Cody observes, "From the evidently chaotic flux of her inner experience she was able to pluck out and transfix the most elusive and transitory sensations and dynamisms."[14] Such crystalline insight demonstrated a sophisticated method of analysis, an analysis that, Cody says, "Freud was not to approach for another half century."[15] The themes of her poetry do not always leap immediately to the eye, and sometimes Dickinson packs layer upon layer, theme upon theme, into a few lines. Richard Sewall, a noted Dickinson biographer, describes this dilemma in his essay "Teaching Dickinson: Testimony of a Veteran": "The first editors in the 1890s divided the poems into four categories—Life, Love, Nature, Time and Eternity,—but ever since then those distinctions have been breaking down as we become more sensitive to the implications of her metaphoric way of thinking." Indeed, says Sewall, "In a single poem, she may be directing her thought to all four."[16] In 1965, Albert Gelpi published a critical study, *Emily Dickinson: The Mind of the Poet*, in which he inventoried approximately forty significant themes.[17]

In studying Dickinson's work, each reader undergoes a unique experience as the nineteenth-century words suddenly spring alive from the page. Dickinson's words touch us today because they address the concerns most central to all human beings: life, love, renunciation, love of nature, death, and the question of immortality. Each of these themes Dickinson explored minutely, at times whimsically, at times holding back no observation, no matter how personal or painful, that would address the subjects she set herself to examine.

Life

Dickinson spent her whole life investigating life itself. Often she expressed her deductions in firm declarations (as in 677):

> To be alive—is Power—
> Existence—in itself—
> Without a further function—
> Omnipotence—Enough—

Simply experiencing the act of being alive brings her a sense of sovereignty quite satisfying in and of itself. Although locked into a world of traditional roles and what we would consider today to be a restrictive pattern of living for an intelligent and inquisitive woman, Dickinson finds gratification in her own vitality. However, after declaring that life itself is "Omnipotence—Enough—," Dickinson lays out a purpose for each of us (680):

> Each Life Converges to some Centre—
> Expressed—or still—
> Exists in every Human Nature
> A Goal—

That we may never reach the goal does not daunt the author, because the afterlife affords us another chance:

> Ungained—it may be—by a Life's low Venture—
> But then—
> Eternity enable the endeavoring
> Again.

The construction of a good life Dickinson likens to building a house (1142):

> The Props assist the House
> Until the House is built
> And then the Props withdraw
> And adequate, erect,
> The House support itself
> And cease to recollect
> The Auger and the Carpenter—
> Just such a retrospect
> Hath the perfected Life—
> A past of Plank and Nail
> And slowness—then the Scaffolds drop
> Affirming it a Soul.

In each of the preceding poems, Dickinson does indeed speak of life, but in each case also she blends the idea of religion, finding one very nearly unexplainable without reference to the other. The precariousness of existence at times gnaws at her, and she demonstrates an unease, wrestling with the idea that living means teetering on the brink of a primeval void (1712):

> A Pit—but Heaven over it—
> And Heaven beside, and Heaven abroad;
> And yet a Pit—
> With Heaven over it.
>
> To stir would be to slip—
> To look would be to drop—
> To dream—to sap the Prop
> That holds my chances up.
> Ah! Pit! With Heaven over it!
>
> The depth is all my thought—
> I dare not ask my feet—
> 'Twould start us where we sit
> So straight you'd scarce suspect
> It was a Pit—with fathoms under it

Its Circuit just the same
Seed—summer—tomb—
Whose Doom to whom

Joanne Feit Diehl describes the hazardous journey of the persona who tries to maintain an equilibrium between heaven and the abyss: "The circuit of the pit (the path around it) is marked by the stages of life: the seed = birth, summer = maturity and the tomb of death. The cycle of life itself walks on the edge," says Diehl, "with no possibility of escape except a heaven that remains tantalizingly beside, abroad, and above it." In this situation, the persona's life is marked not with elation and a joyous moving forward toward salvation; instead, "The depth is all my thought—." Thus, says Diehl, "she is left with awe and the abyss, extremes that cause her to guard each step she takes as she rounds the circle." The abyss itself, harrowing though it may be, attracts Dickinson throughout her life. She dips into and out of the chasm, "the deeper part of the mind," declares Diehl, "to which she descends and from which she emerges through the act of writing poems."[18] The abyss that threatens existence, then, is a focal point of Dickinson's poetic genius.

Love

Love, the essence of human sensibility, flows from Dickinson's work. Whether she examines a bit of grass, the face of a loved one, or an essential connection with the universe, she puts into language the wonder and appreciation experienced by us all, and she captures fleeting thoughts, recording them as a testament to the universality of human existence. "Love is no small, containable thing in Dickinson's poetry," says Jeanne E. Clark; "it is, instead, 'all.' As such, love occupies many different categories, and Dickinson presented multiple kinds of love, often in the same poem."[19] In Poem 164, Dickinson used a metaphor of love found in nature to describe an equal measure of human love:

Mama never forgets her birds,
Though in another tree—
She looks down just as often
And just as tenderly
As when her little mortal nest

With cunning care she wove—
If either of her "sparrows fall,"
She "notices," above.

Clark describes Dickinson's varied treatment of the theme of love: "love as myth; forbidden love; love as paradise; and love as Calvary .... Love becomes multiple, operating as part of the larger metaphor of life's infinitude."[20] Likening all mortal love to that which she saw in a higher power, Dickinson writes (673):

The Love a Life can show Below
Is but a filament, I know,
Of that diviner thing
That faints upon the face of Noon—
And smites the Tinder in the Sun—
And hinders Gabriel's wing—

As her thinking about love matured and her poetry evolved, Dickinson believed that the two were connected, and both were inextricable from divinity (1247):

To pile like Thunder to its close
Then crumble grand away
While Everything created hid
This—would be Poetry—

Or Love—the two coeval come—
We both and neither prove—
Experience either and consume—
For None See God and live—

This poem illustrates the thrust of Dickinson's development and the multilayered nature of her expression as she explores what to her is the sum and substance of living. "Love cannot be finally fixed in Dickinson's poetry," explains Clark. "Not an end in itself, love is a tool—and Poem is its name—something that can be transmuted for excavating, explaining, and embracing the world."[21] Dickinson extrapolates in her fertile mind the building blocks of daily life and relationships into the basis upon which the building blocks of eternity rest.

Always questioning motives, Dickinson enumerates reasons for love in a poem reminiscent of Elizabeth Barrett Browning's "How Do I Love Thee?" (480):

> "Why do I love" You, Sir?
> Because—
> The Wind does not require the Grass
> To answer—Wherefore when He pass
> She cannot keep Her place.
>
> Because He knows—and
> Do not You—
> And We know not—
> Enough for Us
> The Wisdom it be so—
>
> The Lightning—never asked an Eye
> Wherefore it shut—when He was by—
> Because He knows it cannot speak—
> And reasons not contained—
> —Of Talk—
> There be—preferred by Daintier Folk—
>
> The Sunrise—Sir—compelleth Me—
>
> Because He's Sunrise—and I see—
> Therefore—Then—
> I love Thee—

The constancy of love also surfaces in Dickinson's poems. Whether speaking of her own life or discussing an ideal, she articulates the steadfastness of her ideas (549):

> That I did always love
> I bring thee Proof
> That till I loved
> I never lived—Enough—

That I shall love always—
I argue thee
That love is life—
And life hath Immortality—

In this last poem Dickinson demonstrates again the inextricable qualities that she lives by: that love is necessary to life ("till I loved/I never lived—Enough—"); that "love is life"; that both love and life are immortal. She also explores the intensity of love, examining feelings of violent assault on the senses such as "Struck … Maimed … Robbed by" (925):

Struck, was I, not yet by Lightning—
Lightning—lets away
Power to perceive His Process
With Vitality.

Maimed—was I—yet not by Venture—
Stone of stolid Boy—
Nor a Sportsman's Peradventure—
Who mine Enemy?

Robbed—was I—intact to Bandit—
All my Mansion torn—
Sun—withdrawn to Recognition—
Furthest shining—done—

The tumult of spirit resulting from the attacks, however, does not cause Dickinson's persona unease. Indeed, as she continues the poem, she exults in the experience (925):

Yet was not the foe—of any—
Not the smallest Bird
In the nearest Orchard dwelling
Be of Me—afraid.

Most—I love the Cause that slew Me.
Often as I die
Its beloved Recognition
Holds a Sun on Me—

Best—at Setting—as is Nature's—
Neither witnessed Rise
Till the infinite Aurora
In the other's eyes.

Dickinson describes here a familiar adage of love: feeling complete in the presence of one upon whom "the sun rises and sets."

From her earliest years until her death, love represented the entirety of meaning to Dickinson, the complicated weaving of the fabric of life and afterlife. In those moments of contemplation, alone in her room, Dickinson listed, dissected, analyzed, conjectured, yearned, and turned her soul inside out, discovering and defining the infinite shades of meaning of one single word: "That Love is all there is,/Is all we know of Love" (1765).

Renunciation

Renunciation, another of Dickinson's themes, originated from her extensive knowledge of the Bible. Indeed, says Jack Capps, "biblical quotations in her letters and poems far exceed references to any other source or author."[22] Dickinson explores such sacrifice (527):

To put this World down, like a Bundle—
And walk steady, away,
Requires Energy—possibly Agony—
'Tis the Scarlet way
Trodden with straight renunciation
By the Son of God—

Acknowledgment of renunciation became the hallmark of her life, but her own denials most often carried personal benefit. Renouncing the conventional path of marriage and children, Dickinson opened up other avenues that allowed her to devote her energies to poetry. Avoiding a life of public involvement, Dickinson carved more hours out of the day to practice her craft. Deliberately deciding to eschew extensive publication, she retained control of her voluminous work. Also, some of the most controversial instances of renunciation revolve around speculation of Dickinson's possible romantic interludes. "Some degree of deferment or yearning is a common theme in Dickinson's poems, and the language thrives under her mastery of anticipation, possibility, and unquenched desire," says Carolyn Kemp.[23] Dickinson writes around 1863 (745):

> Renunciation—is a piercing Virtue—
> The letting go
> A Presence—for an Expectation—
> Not now—

And the following year (853):

> When One has given up One's life
> The parting with the rest
> Feels easy, as when Day lets go
> Entirely the West
>
> The Peaks, that lingered last
> Remain in Her regret
> As scarcely as the Iodine
> Upon the Cataract.

This last poem seems to define a personal philosophy: once the speaker makes up her mind, she apparently sees no virtue in regrets; once a course has been plotted, the residue of her decision is as fleeting as stray rays of sunshine briefly glancing upon the water. Renunciation, in typical Dickinson expression, both depletes and fulfills.

Love of Nature

The theme of love of nature in all its forms permeates Dickinson's writing. She followed the changing of New England's seasons, exulting in the bounty of harvests, the fierceness of winter storms, the promise of spring, the languor of hot summer days. An ardent botanist, she catalogued flowers around 1845, at about the age of fifteen, in a herbarium that is now the property of the Houghton Library, Harvard University.[24] Her work shows a balance of texture and minute attention to detail. Some of her poems show a similar straightforward natural simplicity (19):

A sepal, petal, and a thorn
Upon a common summer's morn—
A flask of Dew—A Bee or two—
A Breeze—a caper in the trees—
And I'm a Rose!

Similarly, in Poem 986, "A narrow Fellow in the Grass," in which she describes a meeting with a snake, an unusual subject at the time for a poem, Dickinson's persona remarks, "Several of Nature's People/I know, and they know me—/I feel for them a transport/Of cordiality—." Her feelings toward snakes, however, are not quite so cordial: "But never met this Fellow/Attended, or alone/Without a tighter breathing/And Zero at the Bone." Her conscious antipathy toward the snake becomes a part of her description of nature, and her facility for words, even the coining of expressions, allows us to share her shuddering moment of recognition. As she continued to grow in intellectual stature, Dickinson began to see in nature the intimate connection to God and the hope of humanity for an afterlife.

Dickinson's love of nature painted a tremendously complex picture as she tried to find in the natural world a firm understanding of the relationship between people and God and the solutions to questions of shape and continuity of the universe that she could find nowhere in her background. Says Jane Donahue Eberwein, "Poems classified by editors as dealing with 'Nature' can generally be read equally well as speculations on 'Time and Eternity.'"[25] By examining what she saw and analyzing her feelings, just as she had in the rendezvous with the snake, Dickinson drew from within herself the essence of her burgeoning beliefs. These beliefs, however, were tentative and always open to more speculation. Eberwein writes, "In using nature imagery to probe death's mysteries and the prospect of immortality, however, Dickinson avoided easy assurances, either the sentimentally romantic ones of feminine verse or the Christian ones she had been taught to expect."[26] Here Dickinson places herself in a landscape that at once refers to the natural and the supernatural worlds (721):

Behind Me—dips Eternity—
Before Me—Immortality—
Myself—the Term between—
Death but the Drift of Eastern Gray,

Dissolving into Dawn away,
Before the West begin—

"This superbly terrifying poem," says Cynthia Griffin Wolff in her Dickinson biography, "opens with what appears to be a precise set of distinctions that define the relationship between the immanent world and the transcendent."[27] "Eternity" differs from "Immortality," says Wolff, because Immortality promises a life of "integral consciousness," whereas Eternity is "coldly indifferent to the existence of both mankind and God." The second stanza of the poem shows only bleak possibility: "'Tis Kingdoms—afterward—they say—/In perfect—pause-less Monarchy—." Only God "In Duplicate divine," moreover, peoples this Monarchy—there is no sign of souls. Of this spectre, Wolff asks, "Can *God's* consciousness give some shape to 'Immortality' that will be meaningful to human beings, then, or does the reiteration of the Deity merely coil back upon itself like a series of concentric circles, endlessly expanding and yet always arrayed about the same minute center?"[28] The speaker, suspended between two insurmountable forces, then becomes caught up in a despairing tornado of darkness, helplessness, and loss:

'Tis Miracle before Me—then—
'Tis Miracle behind—between—
A Crescent in the Sea—
With Midnight to the North of Her—
And Midnight to the South of Her—
And Maelstrom—in the Sky—

"No powerful pattern of consciousness has succeeded in converting 'Eternity' into 'Immortality,'" says Wolff, whereupon "the first person speaker utterly evaporates" as water and darkness roil, "absorbing human consciousness into oblivion."[29] No picture of supportive, soothing Mother Nature resides here. Dickinson confronts her hope of eternal life in light of her fears of eternal nothingness. "Often Dickinson captures the frustrations of our longing to believe in a Divinity Who works through nature to bless and comfort His children," says Wolff. "Even more often," Wolff continues, "she depicts nature's intrinsic violence in order to expose God's duplicity and extract the *correct* emblematic significance. And in all of these endeavors, she is constrained to work at the very boundaries of human understanding."[30]

Dickinson's views of religion, anchored in the Calvinism of her ancestors and enlightened by the Transcendentalists of her time, then sieved through her own reasoning, show a mind aching for concrete endings to arduous but ethereal mental journeys.

Death and Immortality

Dickinson is famous for her poems dealing with the theme of death and immortality, the most mysterious of human experiences. Before the days of penicillin and other miracle drugs, death lurked behind the most innocent sniffle and occupied the thoughts of everyone to an extent that we cannot comprehend in today's world of medical advancements. The letters of the Dickinson family refer constantly to matters of health and contain firm injunctions and prescriptions for insurance against and treatment of illnesses. On Christmas Eve in 1851, when Austin is away from home teaching at a school for boys in Boston, Emily sends him advice on the treatment of his bout of neuralgia: "I think that warmth and rest, cold water and care, are the best medicines for it.... I cant come, I have no horse to fetch me, I can only advise you of what I think is good, and ask you if you will do it."[31] The Dickinson family was extraordinarily lucky because all three of the children grew to adulthood. However, just as women were expected to care for the ill, so too they were often present at the time of death of a loved one or other member of the community, and the Dickinson women experienced a number of such occurrences. Dickinson describes sharing that last moment in the voice of a spectator (547):

> I've seen a Dying Eye
> Run round and round a Room—
> In search of Something—as it seemed—
> Then Cloudier become—
> And then—obscure with Fog—
> And then—be soldered down
> Without disclosing what it be
> 'Twere blessed to have seen—

In this poem, Dickinson reports the circumstance in a fairly abstract manner: we do not know who is dying; we just witness the process as the poet reveals the steps of her thinking. As life ebbs, the Eye "obscure with Fog," becomes "soldered down," sealed irrevocably before the onlooker can gain a hint of the "Something" that the Eye seeks and may have found. No matter how close or how loved, the poet cannot bridge with the dying person the gap between awareness of life and knowledge of death, cannot fathom the impact of the moment on the person so intimately involved. "Twere blessed to have seen" could refer to either the participant or to the spectator, or both—and to the reader who experiences the scene vicariously.

Arguably, Dickinson's most well known poem discussing death is Poem 712:

> Because I could not stop for Death—
> He kindly stopped for me—
> The Carriage held but just Ourselves
> And Immortality.

In six stanzas, Dickinson, as the persona of the dead, takes the reader on a carriage ride (possibly expanding on the "Something" of her earlier poem) from the world of concrete, everyday activity to the ephemeral world of eternity.

> We passed the School, where Children strove
> At Recess—in the Ring—
> We passed the Fields of Gazing Grain....

Do the dead look at grain, or vice versa? How would we know? Dickinson begins her poem by crossing over space and ends her poem in an analysis of time:

> Since then—'tis Centuries—and yet
> Feels shorter than the Day
> I first surmised the Horses' Heads
> Were toward Eternity—

This juxtaposition of time, space, and exploration of the placing of the human mind at the junction of the two demonstrates the depth of Dickinson's intellect and her ability to investigate the unknown with a sense of purpose and an ensuing sense of personal discovery. In her poetry, she scrutinizes those discoveries and records them for her reader to discover as well, although the course of study may not be easy. As such, this study must include the form of the elegy, which lauds and laments a person after his death, and the elegiac poem, which demonstrates the inward concentration of meditation. Dickinson, says Polish translator Agnieszka Salska, can be placed "much closer to twentieth-century elegists than to the elegiac mode of her own times" because she does not necessarily seek a consolation in death. Instead, says Salska, Dickinson's poems "are hardly 'lamenting' or 'grieving,' for they treat loss as the experiential given and strive, often with alarming curiosity, 'To note the fashions—of the Cross—/And how they're mostly worn—' (561)."[32]

The hushed moment of death and the possibilities of a hereafter engrossed Dickinson and led to a lifetime of examination. Her early religious training guaranteed the faithful a place in Heaven. In around 1859, Dickinson writes (79):

Going to Heaven!
I don't know when—
Pray do not ask me how!
Indeed I'm too astonished
To think of answering you!
Going to Heaven!
How dim it sounds!
And yet it will be done
As sure as flocks go home at night
Unto the Shepherd's arm!

Here the poet speaks words of certainty of an event that has not yet happened but that cannot possibly fail, a going forth to a predetermined and vouched-for destination. When we compare this poem with the following, however, the certainty wavers, and the poet displays her ever-questioning nature (959):

A loss of something ever felt I—
The first that I could recollect
Bereft I was—of what I knew not
Too young that any should suspect
A Mourner walked among the children
I notwithstanding went about

As one bemoaning a Dominion
Itself the only Prince cast out—

Elder, Today, a session wiser
And fainter, too, as Wiseness is—
I find myself still softly searching
For my Delinquent Palaces—

And a Suspicion, like a Finger
Touches my forehead now and then
That I am looking oppositely
For the site of the Kingdom of Heaven—

This poem was written around 1864; Dickinson was about thirty-four years old and at a peak in her writing career. No longer is the destination accepted in the guaranteed version—and Dickinson no longer relies on pat answers to questions of spirituality. "My Business is Circumference," Dickinson writes to T. W. Higginson in July 1868 (L268). Her statement follows the writing of Poem 378: "I saw no Way—The Heavens were stitched—." Possibly a description of the limitations of Calvinism, the poem continues:

I felt the Columns close—
The Earth reversed her Hemispheres—
I touched the Universe—

Here perhaps Dickinson sees her everyday world, steeped in dogma, turned upside down:

And back it slid—and I alone—
A Speck upon a Ball—
Went out upon Circumference—
Beyond the Dip of Bell—

Alone in her understanding, removed from the congregation, Dickinson seems to experience an expansion of spirit that grants to her knowledge of a boundless Universe, unfettered by the strictures of church. For the rest of her life, Dickinson continues to explore her ideas of spirituality and immortality in her poetry and letters. Upon the death of her beloved nephew, Gilbert Dickinson, who died at the age of eight of typhoid fever, Emily writes Poem (1564) to his mother:

> Without a speculation, our little Ajax spans the whole—
>
> Pass to thy Rendezvous of Light,
> Pangless except for us—
> Who slowly ford the Mystery
> Which thou hast leaped across!

Dickinson's concept of afterlife has lost its appellation of "Heaven" and becomes less a haven of hope in the arms of a heavenly father than a realm of enlightenment attained after a period of unknown.

SYMBOLS

As Dickinson perfected her art, she developed a symbolism far beyond the simplistic dove as a symbol of peace or the lamb of God as a symbol of a child so prevalent in the literature of the day. Dickinson grappled with her themes and chose symbols representative of the complexity of her thinking, some of them clear, some obscure, some incomprehensible to a casual reader. The poet often uses small members of the world of nature as her symbols; for instance, the spider—that marvel of dogged perseverance and industry who spins ephemeral reality until its last minute of life—becomes for Dickinson a symbol of her own life and poetic output. She consciously overturns the character of the creature as popularly seen: an offense to good housekeeping or a sly, tempting catcher of unwary "flies"—another symbol, that of foolish sinners. Dickinson's spider "His Yarn of Pearl—unwinds—" just as she unwinds words upon a page stuck together with dashes of cobwebs. Even the most meticulous housekeeper rigorously wielding a broom cannot contend with the artistic spider "dancing softly to Himself" as he "Supplants our Tapestries with His—." With these images Dickinson may be describing her own activities, outwitting the Puritan work ethic to weave her web of words, as much an intrinsic part of her nature as constructing the pattern of crystal thread is to the spider. Barton Levi St. Armand describes Dickinson's spider as "a pagan artificer in an orthodox Christian world ... playful and much too self-indulgent for Puritan economy to tolerate, an aesthete who juggles worlds for his own amusement."[33] Furthermore, says St. Armand, the spider "must pay the penalty of seeing both himself and his art swept away into the abyss of time," to "dangle from the Housewife's Broom—/His Sophistries—forgot—."[34] In this image, Dickinson as the spider-poet realizes, continues St. Armand, that her words—her art—could be destroyed by the reality of death.[35] In a later poem, "A Spider sewed at Night" (1138), Dickinson reflects her own steadfast determination:

> A Spider sewed at Night
> Without a Light
> Upon an Arc of White

This scene could represent a poet alone and working ("in isolation and obscurity," says St. Armand). She questions the substance of her work:

> If Ruff it was of Dame
> Or Shroud of Gnome
> Himself himself inform.

Here we have two more symbols: are her words worthy of notice or comic, misshapen nothings? The answer, states St. Armand, is part of her mystery: "Whether she herself was to be considered a grand dame of poetry or an impish freak of letters was part of her equivocal legacy to posterity."[36] The last line of the stanza represents Dickinson's philosophy: whatever the outcome, the spider-poet constructs himself as he constructs his art.

Flowers figure prominently in Dickinson's work, and the daisy in particular she uses as a symbol of seeming innocence (106):

> The Daisy follows soft the Sun—
> And when his golden walk is done—
> Sits shyly at his feet—
> He—waking—finds the flower there—
> Wherefore—Marauder—art thou here?
> Because, Sir, love is sweet!

In this section of Poem 106 we have the floral symbol of a shy, adoring girl who follows the object of her love "soft"—without intruding on him. She sits patiently until he wakes—following his schedule, not interfering with his rhythm, enduring even name calling—all in the name of love that is revealing in its conventional naivete.

Several images emerge when Dickinson writes of volcanoes—symbols of creative force, passion, and inhibited expression. In Poem 601 "A still—Volcano—Life—," Dickinson writes in a restrained, contradictory manner of a seething possibility of eruption that "flickered in the night"—possibly representing Dickinson herself and her writing—and, moreover, an earthquake "too subtle to suspect," images of contained and controlled power not generally noticed. These images perhaps explain the necessity to restrain and conceal the power and meaning of her words, which would perhaps not be welcomed were they known. Poem 1677 also discloses a volatile inner being:

> On my volcano grows the Grass
> A meditative spot—
> An acre for a Bird to choose
> Would be the General thought—
>
> How red the Fire rocks below—
> How insecure the sod
> Did I disclose
> Would populate with awe my solitude.

The persona of this poem understands very well the power within and at the moment has complete control of that power.

Indeed, in her later years, Dickinson became more symbol herself than ordinary person. Her idiosyncrasies are legendary and perplexing: Why did she always wear white? Why did she remain a recluse? Why did she receive company at times from behind a partially open door? Why did she seem to correspond in riddles? Biographers and other scholars often spend hundreds of hours trying to decipher the poem that Emily Dickinson fashioned of her life.

Dickinson's Language and Style: Forging Tools to Construct Meaning

Working as she did in near solitude for over thirty years, Dickinson virtually constructed her own language, a language that both intrigues and puzzles readers. Discarding the usual rules of English, Dickinson refashioned ordinary words to extraordinary purpose and sometimes even invented new words when she found none to suffice. The language that Dickinson constructed enabled her to express herself in her time in history. Cristanne Miller describes the writer's need: "Dickinson writes as she does because of a combination of factors: her belief in the extraordinary power of language, her responses to the language she reads in mid-nineteenth century America, and her sense of herself as woman and poet."[37] Using Miller's three topics as a bare outline, I provide an independent interpretation of Dickinson's use of language and the unique style of poetry that her language develops.

Dickinson's belief in the power of language arises logically from her background. As the daughter of a lawyer in a well-educated family, as one who had studied the classics, including classical argument, and as an intelligent and astute individual, Dickinson absorbed an exceptional academic attitude and developed her education without pause throughout her life. Much has been written of her vast knowledge of the Bible and Shakespeare, her love of the meter of the hymns of Isaac Watts, and her use of Noah Webster's Dictionary and the Lexicography—all of these sources provided for Dickinson a solid base upon which to build. (Benjamin Lease notes Dickinson's "passionate involvement with Thomas à Kempis."[38]) In addition, her love of British poetry and enjoyment of American writers published in magazines, newspapers, and books showed her avid interest in daily life. Although her lively and vocal behavior during childhood did change to a reclusive, contemplative mode of living in later years, her reliance on language continued, enforced by the developing of her art as she wove words into new meaning that demonstrated the strength of her talent and the power of her purpose. Edward Dickinson controlled the language in his household, and the voice of authority was the primary characteristic of that language. "No one opposed his decisions," says Millicent Todd Bingham, "least of all his family."[39] The family did not indulge in mutual chatter, lightly commingling their ideas. Bingham relates the atmosphere of the Dickinson "citadel": "You were bound to those to whom you gave loyalty and devotion, but with whom you did not share your thoughts. In this, as in all things, Edward Dickinson set the pattern. With the members of the family he shared everything except his soul."[40] This reluctance to speak outwardly of inner matters may have caused Emily to refine her language later to express on paper what she could not say out loud and to appropriate for herself the voice of authority.

The written language of the nineteenth century was distinctly engendered: men traditionally wrote of politics, law, philosophy, and the public good; women traditionally wrote of home and hearth, piety, submissiveness, gentility, romance, and sentimentality. Although the Dickinsons spoke to one another with reserve, they read constantly and from a variety of sources and paid eager attention to the happenings of their community, the country, and the world. Newspapers and magazines provided information on current events as well as literary offerings. The Dickinsons were intimates of many people in literary circles. The editor of the *Springfield Republican*, Samuel Bowles, and the editor of *Scribner's Monthly Magazine*, Josiah Holland, were close family friends; the Dickinson family read both their publications avidly, as well as the *Atlantic Monthly*, which featured purely literary pieces. The family also bought, borrowed, and lent books constantly. St. Armand observes that this appetite for contemporary reading is often minimized by critics but should not be ignored: Emily Dickinson's "taste for sentimental, sensational, and Gothic narratives has been usually brushed aside as an embarrassing aberration, yet this taste pervaded her sensibility and endured until the end of her life."[41] Nineteenth century philosophies also intrigued Dickinson. As a young woman of twenty, she began to read the essays and poems of Transcendentalists, especially Emerson and his student, Henry David Thoreau. At approximately this time in her life, Dickinson began to find poetry within herself, some of it expressed in language that showed her increasing preoccupation with life and truth: "I like a look of Agony,/Because I know it's true—" (241).

Although Dickinson often wrote in the meter of hymns and sometimes slid into sentimentality, she also altered language as she explored her growth as a woman and taught herself to write, structuring her poems and honing her style by restructuring language to suit her need. In Poem 1331, Dickinson lays out two definitions of words, assigning gender and rank:

Wonder—is not precisely Knowing
And not precisely Knowing not—
A beautiful but bleak condition
He has not lived who has not felt—

Suspense—is his maturer Sister—
Whether Adult Delight is Pain
Or of itself a new misgiving—
This is the Gnat that mangles men—

Here Dickinson assigns a "beautiful but bleak condition" to a young male and appropriates for the feminine voice adulthood and maturity—allowing that such elevated status must deal with more complicated issues and consequences.

Poem 1295 deals with time and space, an unusual combination of subjects for a nineteenth century female writer:

Two Lengths has every Day—
Its absolute extent
And Area superior
By Hope or Horror lent—

The last line of the stanza infuses the measure of space—"Area"—with the personal feelings that make all lengths of time relative. These four lines place Dickinson squarely in the philosopher's seat. Her need to inspect, to analyze, and to judge for herself all facets of life shows a grasp of autonomy and authority not prevalent in literature written by women of the period. We can gauge a measure of her accomplishment when we read that one of her few published poems, "Success is counted Sweetest" (67) was popularly attributed to Emerson.[42]

When we read Dickinson's uniquely constructed language, we are aware that it developed a style unlike that of any other poet. Of course, we note her use of punctuation, primarily the famous dash. Dickinson's eccentric, nontraditional punctuation at first startled her readers. Editors of original publications of her poetry "corrected" her punctuation, often altering the poet's meaning and substance. Later scholars, however, began to insist that Dickinson's use or lack of punctuation was a conscious construction central to her work, and her poems were then printed intact, with variant words included in the most elaborate texts. Dickinson chose words with great deliberation, skewing grammar to fit design. "The unusual sound of her language," says Miller, "stems from the transposition of classes of words ... a verb is used as a noun, for example, without a change in its form." At times, Miller continues, "action becomes object": for instance, "Piles of solid Moan—" (639).[43] The complexity of Dickinson's form emerged as she hammered words to rearrange meaning, forging, according to Adrienne Rich, "a language more varied, more compressed, more dense with implications, more complex of syntax, than any American poetic language to date."[44]

Dickinson was conscious that she spoke not only for herself but also for those who had not her voice, embodying "the ancient concept of the poet," as Rich explains, "which is that she is endowed to speak for those who do not have the gift of language, or to see for those who—for whatever reason—are less conscious of what they are living through."[45] As she moved through the stages of philosophical growth, Dickinson followed her conviction to find her Truth, but, unable to speak freely, she also followed her own advice and told it "slant." The humor, irony, and satire that demonstrate Dickinson's wit and depth of intellect we may have expected, but Jay Leyda has named her most notable stylistic device the "omitted center."[46] The necessity of speaking is hampered by the need to avoid the confrontation of truth, and so the poem travels on the "circumference" of the subject without clearly enhancing the reader's understanding of the point. In these instances, says Joanne Dobson, the reader may benefit from analyzing the style of the poem, rather than the meaning, "to determine the significance of the impediments to comprehension."[47]

Many theories have been suggested for the ambiguity and confusion that abound in Dickinson's work, such as a lost love and religious upheaval; she chose to relay those volcanic disturbances in a language of mystery. Even her command of language and her facility for shaping it to her needs were often not enough to satisfy Dickinson. Harold Bloom explains her frustration: "Better perhaps than any other poet, she knows and indicates that what is worth representing is beyond depiction, what is worth saying cannot be said."[48] Just as Plato insists that writing itself is only a poor imitation of a poet's words, Dickinson understands—and laments—that words are only a poor imitation of a poet's thoughts. Perhaps closely examining Dickinson's style, her *use* of words, can give us a better picture of the workings of her mind than can the words themselves.

Whatever themes we identify, whatever symbols we categorize in Dickinson's poems, regardless of whether we understand precisely what Dickinson intends to say, one overall concept remains inescapable: speaking in her own voice or in other personas, Dickinson speaks the language of truth as her ethics demand. Gudrun Grabher, Roland Hagenbuchle, and Cristanne Miller, editors of *The Emily Dickinson Handbook*, offer a reference to the work of Fatima Falih Ahmed Al-Bedrani of the University of Baghdad for a recent view of Dickinson's themes: "She expresses the deepest feelings of the soul of man.... Emily Dickinson recognizes two moments in life as being crucial, or, as she defines them, 'sacramental': the moment of love and the moment of death ... [which] opens another and better life as immortality, which is her third significant theme." Al-Bedrani emphasizes, "One can say that no other poet has written on such a variety of themes as Emily Dickinson did. Yet beneath all, truth is the motif."[49] This passion for truth, however, does not always come to us in a clear manner. The truth of Dickinson's life and art may not have been easy to express or prudent to champion in her home or community. Nevertheless, she found a way to be faithful to herself: "Tell all the Truth but tell it slant—" she says. "The Truth must dazzle gradually/Or every man be blind—" (1129). Rich gives us an explanation from her own perspective as a female poet: "It is always what is under pressure in us, especially under pressure of concealment—that explodes in poetry." Dickinson, says Rich, had to "retranslate her own unorthodox, subversive, sometimes volcanic propensities into a dialect called metaphor: her native language." Dickinson tells "all the Truth," but she does so in language and style that both offers and withholds meaning, titillating scholars who are sure that they have cracked Dickinson's code—until another interpretation follows a different "slant."

Life Informing Art, and Vice Versa

During the twentieth century, some theorists insisted that each work of literature stood isolated, removed from its historical significance and from the life of the artist who produced it. Current thinking, however, leads us to examine closely the life and times of literary artists to search their life experiences, identifying those factors that produce their art, to find within their words what has informed their lives; Emily Dickinson is a prime subject of such study. Theodora Ward expresses the connection between poet and poem:

> Whether or not the subject matter of a poem deals with circumstances of time and place, the poet himself speaks through it. He not only shows his conscious attitudes, but inevitably reveals something of his unconscious mind, both on a personal level and on the deeper one that touches his relation to those underlying psychological patterns common to all men."[50]

Dickinson struggled with her psychological demons on a daily basis, as do most people. We, however, are fortunate enough to have the bulk of her life's thought processes laid before us as a whole. We can trace the maturing of her thinking parallel with the development of her art. Through the existing correspondence, we can glimpse the mundane as well as the dramatic happenings in her life, and because of the intense scholarship devoted to her history, we can approximate the dates of her poems in correlation to those events. We can with increasing accuracy follow Dickinson's emotional upheavals and the resulting changes in her writing. We can hear her own words as she reflects on that writing, and we can observe the subsequent changes in substance and style.

Studying the effects of a writer's work upon his or her own subsequent writing is new territory in the realm of critical investigation. Harold Bloom suggests, "A writer's influence upon himself or herself is an unexplored problem in criticism" (hence this volume) and that some great literary figures, such as Dickinson, Wallace Stevens, Willa Cather, and Emily Brontë, "seem to have had so little of the full intensity of life when compared to the vitality of their work, that we might almost speak of the work in the work, rather than even the work in a person."[51] Considering Dickinson's life in the acerbic, restrained, restricted household to which she was welded, by custom and by choice, we can thus picture her ascending the stairs, moving upward in body and spirit, away from proscription and duty, through her bedroom door into a private sanctuary where her "real" world lay, a world of the mind where she could flow as she wished from center to circumference, some days watching her pen identify and overcome her demons in triumph, some days wallowing in the despair of limitless questions, resulting in only hesitant, unsatisfying answers—the life and mind of the poet exposed upon the page.

Nineteenth Century Reception of Dickinson's Poetry

When Dickinson sent copies of several of her poems to Thomas Wentworth Higginson in the spring of 1862, asking for his critique, he suggested that she not think of publishing her work.[52] However, ten of Dickinson's poems did eventually reach an appreciative audience of thousands of readers during her lifetime, with or without her permission. At first puzzled about the author's identity, the reading public gradually became aware that a talented but reclusive poet resided in Amherst. Karen Dandurand's "Dickinson and the Public" provides a detailed description of the scope of circulation possible through publication and reprints in newspapers such as the *Springfield Daily Republican*, *Round Table*, and *Drum Beat* in the 1860s.[53] Newspapers were a popular source of poems, says Dandurand, which readers clipped, copied, pasted in scrapbooks, and shared with friends. Dickinson's anonymous publications garnered enthusiastic followers: John White Chadwick, reviewing *Poems* in 1890, mentions his having "treasured in my memory for more than twenty years" a Dickinson poem previously published in *Round Table*.[54] The poems that Dickinson chose to share with family and friends often found their way to larger groups of contemporaries, because, as previously stated, Dickinson's relationships included many acquaintances in literary circles. Although Higginson initially discouraged Emily from publishing, he changed his mind as he began to appreciate that the strength of original form and the substance of the poems greatly outweighed picayune concerns over perceived irregularities in grammar and punctuation. Higginson read a number of her poems at a meeting of the New England Woman's Club, writing to his sister Anna, "Their weird & strange power excited much interest" (originally quoted by Leyda). Many people, including noted authors, clamored for more poetry from Dickinson. Her contemporary, Helen Hunt Jackson, a great friend of Dickinson, wrote to her on March 20, 1876: "You are a great poet—and it is wrong to the day you live in that you will not sing aloud."

The newspaper report of the poetry reading commented upon the "remarkable strength and originality" of the poet, whom Higginson declined to name.[55] On Dickinson's death, hundreds of the carefully preserved packets containing her poems were released to her grateful editors. Higginson and Mabel Loomis Todd published *Poems*, a short collection of Dickinson's works, in 1890. Two more books followed: the Second Series in 1891 and Third Series in 1896. The total number of volumes sold neared 20,000, an impressive accomplishment and an indication of the strength of public interest.[56] In his essay "An Open Portfolio," Higginson presents approximately a dozen of Dickinson's poems. "Her verses," he says, "are in most cases like poetry plucked up by the roots; we have them with earth, stones, and dew adhering." Contradicting the dismissiveness of his original comments to Emily on the subject of publication, Higginson lauds the very attributes he once deplored, noting that the poems he now champions must be accepted "as they are. Wayward and unconventional in the last degree; defiant of form, measure, rhyme, and even grammar."[57]

Alexander Young reviewed the forthcoming first volume of *Poems* and attested to "their union of profound insight into nature and life with a remarkable vividness of description."[58] Todd lent further support in her column for the Washington, D.C., *Home Magazine*, stating that Dickinson's poems "all reveal the fearless working of a mind that stopped at no conventional barriers."[59] Writing in the *Springfield Republican*, Charles Goodrich Whiting also reviewed *Poems* in a complimentary light: "It is the special and serious revelation of a soul apart, by its own choice, but yet vividly sympathetic with its kind, and cognizant of human experience by its intuitive revelations."[60] And on April 30, 1891, Samuel Barrows described *Poems* as "one of the freshest, most original and suggestive volumes of poetry that has been published in recent years."[61]

Not all reviews were completely favorable, however. The *Manchester Guardian* offered a British point of view by a columnist who was determined to wade through the "almost incredible overpraise with which some American critics bespatter their country and its works" to find the real voice of Dickinson, whose poems were finally pronounced "really remarkable." That praise grew faint a time or two in the article as the writer found Dickinson's metaphorical conceits "sometimes extremely striking" ("Afraid? Of whom am I afraid?") and sometimes "driveling" ("Grand go the years in the crescent above them"). A "blind or careless neglect to complete the form" of the poem "Pain has an element of blank" disturbed the reviewer because that neglect "interferes a little with what is otherwise the strong expression of a true thought."[62]

A disparaging review after the Second Series was published suggested that Higginson and Todd could "no longer count on a generally favorable reception for Dickinson in the editorial rooms of the religious and family weeklies." This article, for which no author was mentioned, warned that Dickinson's "A Prayer" "comes dangerously near" to being irreverent.[63] Another British critic, identified as Andrew Lang, decried Dickinson's popularity in the United States: "She reminds us of no sane nor educated writer." Some of Dickinson's verses he declared "assuredly below contempt"—for instance, "New feet within my garden go."[64] Willis J. Buckingham accords to Thomas Bailey Aldrich the distinction of producing the "best-known—and perhaps most influential—rejection of Dickinson's poetry to appear in the 1890s." Aldrich referred to "three or four bits" of negligible interest in the entire volume of *Poems* (most likely the First Series) but said, "for the most part, the ideas totter and toddle, not having learned to walk." Then Aldrich added a condescending note: "In spite of this, several of the quatrains are curiously touching, they have such a pathetic air of yearning to be poems." Although he admitted to a certain "quality" in the poems, he found that "the incoherence and formlessness of her—I don't know how to designate them—versicles are fatal."[65] In six years' time, the three volumes in the series of *Poems* had elicited from critics as much focus on the reclusive lifestyle of the poet as on the considered analysis of her verse; perhaps the critics recognized that the two topics were intricately linked.

Dickinson and World Literature: Why and How Her Influence Continues

Although Dickinson assured Higginson that her aspirations to publish her poems were as "foreign as firmament to fin," she is nonetheless one of the most studied poets in the world, widely translated, attracting scholars from scores of countries to the meetings of the Emily Dickinson International Society's conferences, the latest of which was held in Trondheim, Norway, in August, 2001. Libraries of books, journal articles, and doctoral dissertations continue to add to the accumulation of interpretation of Dickinson as a poet and a person. Some authors minutely dissect her poems, analyzing meter, trying to understand her meaning; others turn their attention to her private life, questioning her possible romantic attachments and the name of the person whom she addressed as "Master," attempting to plumb the forces that helped shape her life and the reasoning behind her eccentricities. What we guess can never be finally substantiated, of course, but what we see on the printed page provides a link to the poet's mind, a link that many scholars believe was Dickinson's bequest to the world: she spoke not only for herself but for and to everybody. Richard Sewall continues this process of thought, describing a property of Dickinson's lyric poetry in which her writing becomes an intimate communication with the reader. The solitude of the writer is entered on the page, and the page itself then becomes the physical carrier that "substantiates the otherwise purely metaphorical relation between writer and reader. It embodies the separation between their two bodies."[66] This lyrical structure of Dickinson's poems allows millions of her readers to confront themselves and their innermost thoughts. Although they may never be able to articulate their feelings so eloquently, they can recognize themselves in her fascicles. Her wide appeal to international audiences underscores the correctness of Sewall's statements.

Heinz Ickstadt refers to this sphere of Dickinson's poetry as "inwardly directed consciousness" and likens her to the French symbolists such as Beaudelaire and Mallarmé. All three, says Ickstadt, "at the same historical moment, developed a poetic idiom of modernity, and transformed the Christian religion they had inherited into a new secular religion of art and consciousness." Because Dickinson was a woman, however, she added discourse on gender. Rather than trying to isolate a dominant discourse, says Ickstadt, we should "push possible meanings into all directions and fully develop the semantic multiplicity that such overlapping inevitably generates."[67] This multiplicity of speech involving art, consciousness, and gender has now spanned parts of three centuries and impacts the current study of poetry. Regarded with Walt Whitman's work as a primary influence on modern American poetry, Dickinson's work continues to resonate today. Texts of Dickinson's poems and critical responses to those poems are required reading, not only in nineteenth-century literature courses and courses of modern American poetry, but also in women's studies, as well as courses devoted exclusively to the study of Dickinson herself. The secluded, private, introverted works of America's greatest female poet have gone out upon the "Circumference" of the literary world, but her works are not limited just to the scholarly sphere. Dickinson, who sees "New Englandly," touches the thoughts of readers everywhere with the zephyr-like whispers and volcanic thunderings of a kindred spirit, instilling the essence of the human universe into her poetry, and then bequeathing it to all of us.

NOTES

1. All poems herein are numbered after Thomas H. Johnson's editing of *The Complete Poems of Emily Dickinson.* Boston: Little, Brown, 1960.

2. From a definitive biography of Dickinson by George F. Whicher, *This Was A Poet: A Critical Biography of Emily Dickinson.* New York: Charles Scribner's Sons, 1938, p. 165 ff.

3. For a comprehensive compilation of Dickinson's biographers, see Martha Ackman's "Biographical Studies of Dickinson." In Grabher, Gudrun, Roland Hagenbuchle, and Cristanne Miller, eds. *The Emily Dickinson Handbook.* Amherst, Mass.: University of Massachusetts Press, 1998.

4. "(L)" here and throughout refers to Thomas H. Johnson's editing of *Emily Dickinson: Selected Letters,* 9th ed. Cambridge, Mass.: The Belknap Press, Harvard University Press, 1998, p. ix.

5. L13 to Abiah Root.

6. L32 .

7. L52.

8. Poem 111.

9. Bingham, Millicent Todd, ed. *Emily Dickinson's Home: Letters of Edward Dickinson and His Family.* New York: Harper, 1955, p. 117.

10. L36.

11. Bingham, p. 117.

12. Ibid., p. 255.

13,. Ibid., p. 119.

14. Cody, John. *After Great Pain: The Inner Life of Emily Dickinson.* Cambridge, Mass.: Harvard University Press, 1971, p. 6.

15. Ibid., p. 7.

16. Richard Sewall. "Teaching Dickinson: Testimony of a Veteran." Fast and Gordon, pp. 30-32.

17. Gelpi, Albert J. *Emily Dickinson: The Mind of a Poet.* Cambridge, Mass.: Harvard University Press, 1965.

18. See Bloom, Harold, ed. Emerson, Dickinson, and the Abyss. In *Emily Dickinson (Modern Critical Views).* New York: Chelsea House, 1985, pp. 157-158.

19. Eberwein, Jane Donahue, ed. *An Emily Dickinson Encyclopedia.* Westport, Conn.: Greenwood Press, 1998, p. 183.

20. Ibid.

21. Ibid.

22. Capps, Jack L. *Emily Dickinson's Reading, 1836-1886.* Cambridge, Mass.: Harvard University Press, 1966, p. 30.

23. Eberwein, p. 246.

24. Gudrun Grabher, Roland Hagenbuchle, and Cristanne Miller have edited an exhaustive reference book on all aspects of Emily Dickinson's life and works: *The Emily Dickinson Handbook.* Amherst, Mass.: University of Massachusetts Press, 1998. See p. 84.

25. Ibid., p. 205.

26. Ibid., p. 206.

27. Wolff, Cynthia Griffin. *Emily Dickinson.* New York: Alfred A. Knopf, 1986, p. 292.

28. Ibid., p. 293.

29. Ibid., p. 294.

30. Ibid., p. 295.

31. L66.

32. Eberwein, pp. 97-98.

33. St. Armand, Barton Levi. *Emily Dickinson and Her Culture: The Soul's Society.* Cambridge, U.K.: Cambridge University Press, 1984, p. 31.

34. Ibid., p. 33.

35. Ibid., p. 34.

36. Ibid., p. 36.

37. Cristanne Miller. *Emily Dickinson: A Poet's Grammar.* Cambridge, Mass.: Harvard University Press, 1987, p. 1.

38. Benjamin Lease. *Emily Dickinson's Reading of Men and Books: Sacred Soundings.* New York: St. Martin's Press, 1990, p. 8.

39. Bingham, p. 3.

40. Ibid., p. 5.

41. St. Armand,. p. 21

42. L573d. Dickinson's poem appeared in *A Masque of Poets*, published in 1878. Karen Dandurand, in "Dickinson and the Public," mentions that Ralph Waldo Emerson "may have taken a particular interest" in the poem since it was "attributed to him by several reviewers." (In Weisbuch, Robert, and Martin Orzeck, eds. *Dickinson and Audience.* Ann Arbor, Mich.: University of Michigan Press, 1996, p. 258.)

43. Miller, pp. 59-60.

44. Rich, Adrienne. "Vesuvius at Home: The Power of Emily Dickinson." In Sandra M. Gilbert and Susan Gubar, eds. *Shakespeare's Sisters: Feminist Essays on Women Poets.* Bloomington, Ind.: Indiana University Press, 1979, p. 103.

45. Ibid., p. 119.

46. Jay Leyda. *The Years and Hours of Emily Dickinson*, 2 vols. New Haven, Conn.: Yale University Press, 1960, I. xxi.

47. Dobson, Joanne. *Dickinson and the Strategies of Reticence.* Bloomington, Ind.: Indiana University Press, 1989, p.124.

48. Ibid., p. 6.

49. Ibid., p. 187.

50. Ward, Theodora. *The Capsule of the Mind.* Cambridge, Mass.: Belknap Press, Harvard University Press, 1961, p. viii.

51. See Bloom, Harold, "The Work in the Writer," earlier in this book.

52. Dickinson was responding to Higginson's article in the April *Atlantic Monthly*, "Letter to a Young Contributor," giving advice to novice writers.

53. Weisbuch and Orzeck, pp. 255-277. Karen Dandurand has also contributed a significant compilation of books, articles, and dissertations in *Dickinson Scholarship: An Annotated Bibliography, 1969-1985.* New York: Garland Publishing, 1988.

54. Ibid., pp. 258-259

55. Weisbuch and Orzeck, p. 266. (Published in *Woman's Journal*, 15 July 1876.

56. Buckingham, Willis J. *Emily Dickinson's Reception in the 1890s.* Pittsburgh: University of Pittsburgh Press, 1989. This volume lists nearly 600 reviews in detail.

57. Ibid., p. 8.

58. Ibid., p. 9. "Boston Letter." *Critic*, n.s. 14:183-184, October 11, 1890.

59. Ibid., p. 12. Magazine published November 3, 1890, p. 13.

60. Ibid., p. 14. Printed November 16, 1890, p. 4.

61. Ibid., p. 32.

62. Ibid., pp. 161-163. "Books of the Week." August 11, 1891, p. 7.

63. Ibid., p. 316. *Christian Union*, 45:1212, June 18, 1892.

64. Ibid., p. 80. "The Newest Poet." *Daily News* [London], January 2, 1891, p. 5.

65. Ibid., pp. 282-283.

66. Weisbuch and Orzeck, pp. 81-84.

67. *The Emily Dickinson Journal*, 10.1:55-69, 2001.

Works Cited

Bingham, Millicent Todd, ed. *Emily Dickinson's Home: Letters of Edward Dickinson and His Family.* New York: Harper, 1955.

Bloom, Harold, ed. *Emily Dickinson (Modern Critical Reviews).* New York: Chelsea House, 1985.

Buckingham, Willis J. *Emily Dickinson's Reception in the 1890s.* Pittsburgh: University of Pittsburgh Press, 1989.

Capps, Jack L. *Emily Dickinson's Reading, 1836-1886.* Cambridge, Mass.: Harvard University Press, 1966.

Cody, John. *After Great Pain: The Inner Life of Emily Dickinson.* Cambridge, Mass.: Harvard University Press, 1971.

Dandurand, Karen. *Dickinson Scholarship: An Annotated Bibliography, 1969-1985.* New York: Garland Publishing, 1988.

Eberwein, Jane Donahue, ed. *An Emily Dickinson Encyclopedia.* Westport, Conn.: Greenwood Press, 1998.

Gelpi, Albert J. *Emily Dickinson: The Mind of a Poet.* Cambridge, Mass.: Harvard University Press, 1965.

Grabher, Gudrun, Roland Hagenbuchle, and Cristanne Miller, eds. *The Emily Dickinson Handbook.* Amherst, Mass.: University of Massachusetts Press, 1998.

Ickstadt, Heinz. *The Emily Dickinson Journal* 10.1, (2001) 55-69, 2001.

Johnson, Thomas H., ed. *Emily Dickinson: Selected Letters*, 9th ed. Cambridge, Mass.: The Belknap Press, Harvard University Press, 1998.

Johnson, Thomas H., ed. *The Complete Poems of Emily Dickinson*. Boston: Little, Brown, 1960.

Lease, Benjamin. *Emily Dickinson's Reading of Men and Books: Sacred Soundings*. New York: St. Martin's Press, 1990.

Miller, Cristanne. *Emily Dickinson: A Poet's Grammar*. Cambridge, Mass.: Harvard University Press, 1987.

Rich, Adrienne. "Vesuvius at Home: The Power of Emily Dickinson." In Sandra M. Gilbert and Susan Gubar, eds. *Shakespeare's Sisters: Feminist Essays on Women Poets*. Bloomington, Ind.: Indiana University Press, 1979.

St. Armand, Barton Levi. *Emily Dickinson and Her Culture: The Soul's Society*. Cambridge, U.K.: Cambridge University Press, 1984.

Sewall, Richard B. "Teaching Dickinson: Testimony of a Veteran." From *Approaches to Teaching Dickinson's Poetry*, eds. Robin Riley Fast and Christine M. Gordon. Modern Language Association of America, 1989.

Weisbuch, Robert, and Martin Orzeck, eds. *Dickinson and Audience*. Ann Arbor, Mich.: University of Michigan Press, 1996.

Whicher, George F. *This Was a Poet: A Critical Biography of Emily Dickinson*. New York: Charles Scribner's Sons, 1938.

Wolff, Cynthia Griffin. *Emily Dickinson*. New York: Alfred A. Knopf, 1986.

ADRIENNE RICH

Vesuvius at Home: The Power of Emily Dickinson

I am traveling at the speed of time, along the Massachusetts Turnpike. For months, for years, for most of my life, I have been hovering like an insect against the screens of an existence which inhabited Amherst, Massachusetts, between 1830 and 1886. The methods, the exclusions, of Emily Dickinson's existence could not have been my own; yet more and more, as a woman poet finding my own methods, I have come to understand her necessities, could have been witness in her defense.

"Home is not where the heart is," she wrote in a letter, "but the house and the adjacent buildings." A statement of New England realism, a directive to be followed. Probably no poet ever lived so much and so purposefully in one house; even, in one room. Her niece Martha told of visiting her in her corner bedroom on the second floor at 280 Main Street, Amherst, and of how Emily Dickinson made as if to lock the door with an imaginary key, turned and said: "Matty: here's freedom."

I am traveling at the speed of time, in the direction of the house and buildings.

Western Massachusetts: the Connecticut Valley: a countryside still full of reverberations: scene of Indian uprisings, religious revivals, spiritual confrontations, the blazing-up of the lunatic fringe of the Puritan coal. How peaceful and how threatened it looks from Route 91, hills gently curled above the plain, the tobacco-barns standing in fields

---

sheltered with white gauze from the sun, and the sudden urban sprawl: ARCO, MacDonald's, shopping plazas. The country that broke the heart of Jonathan Edwards, that enclosed skies breaking into warm sunshine, light-green spring softening the hills, dogwood and wild fruit-trees blossoming in the hollows.

From Northampton bypass there's a four-mile stretch of road to Amherst—Route 9—between fruit farms, steakhouses, supermarkets. The new University of Massachusetts rears its skyscrapers up from the plain against the Pelham Hills. There is new money here, real estate, motels. Amherst succeeds on Hadley almost without notice. Amherst is green, rich-looking, secure; we're suddenly in the center of town, the crossroads of the campus, old New England college buildings spread around two village greens, a scene I remember as almost exactly the same in the dim past of my undergraduate years when I used to come there for college weekends.

Left on Seelye Street, right on Main; driveway at the end of a yellow picket fence. I recognize the high hedge of cedars screening the house, because twenty-five years ago I walked there, even then drawn toward the spot, trying to peer over. I pull into the driveway behind a generous nineteenth-century brick mansion with wings and porches, old trees and green lawns. I ring at the back door—the door through which Dickinson's coffin was carried to the cemetery a block away.

For years I have been not so much envisioning Emily Dickinson as trying to visit, to enter her mind, through her poems and letters, and through my own intimations of what it could have meant to be one of the two mid-nineteenth-century American geniuses, and a woman, living in Amherst, Massachusetts. Of the other genius, Walt Whitman, Dickinson wrote that she had heard his poems were "disgraceful." She knew her own were unacceptable by her world's standards of poetic convention, and of what was appropriate, in particular, for a woman poet. Seven were published in her lifetime, all edited by other hands; more than a thousand were laid away in her bedroom chest, to be discovered after her death. When her sister discovered them, there were decades of struggle over the manuscripts, the manner of their presentation to the world, their suitability for publication, the poet's own final intentions. Narrowed down by her early editors and anthologists, reduced to quaintness or spinsterish oddity by many of her commentators, sentimentalized, fallen-in-love-with like some gnomic Garbo, still unread in the breadth and depth of her full range of work, she was, and is, a wonder to me when I try to imagine myself into that mind.

I have a notion that genius knows itself; that Dickinson chose her seclusion, knowing she was exceptional and knowing what she needed. It was, moreover, no hermetic retreat, but a seclusion which included a wide range of people, of reading and correspondence. Her sister Vinnie said, "Emily is always looking for the rewarding person." And she found, at various periods, both women and men: her sister-in-law, Susan Gilbert, Amherst visitors and family friends such as Benjamin Newton, Charles Wadsworth, Samuel Bowles, editor of the Springfield *Republican* and his wife; her friends Kate Anthon and Helen Hunt Jackson, the distant but significant figures of Elizabeth Barrett, the Brontës, George Eliot. But she carefully selected her society and controlled the disposal of her time. Not only the "gentlewomen in plush" of Amherst were excluded; Emerson visited next door but she did not go to meet him; she did not travel or receive routine visits; she avoided strangers. Given her vocation, she was neither eccentric nor quaint; she was determined to survive, to use her powers, to practice necessary economies.

Suppose Jonathan Edwards had been born a woman; suppose William James, for that matter, had been born a woman? (The invalid seclusion of his sister Alice is suggestive.) Even from men, New England took its psychic toll; many of its geniuses seemed peculiar in one way or another, particularly along the lines of social intercourse. Hawthorne, until he married, took his meals in his bedroom, apart from the family. Thoreau insisted on the values both of solitude and of geographical restriction, boasting that "I have travelled much in Concord." Emily Dickinson—viewed by her bemused contemporary Thomas Higginson as "partially cracked," by the twentieth century as fey or pathological—has increasingly struck me as a practical woman, exercising her gift as she had to, making choices. I have come to imagine her as somehow too strong for her environment, a figure of powerful will, not at all frail or breathless, someone whose personal dimensions would be felt in a household. She was her father's favorite daughter though she professed being afraid of him. Her sister dedicated herself to the everyday domestic labors which would free Dickinson to write. (Dickinson herself baked the bread, made jellies and gingerbread, nursed her mother through a long illness, was a skilled horticulturalist who grew pomegranates, calla lilies, and other exotica in her New England greenhouse.)

Upstairs at last: I stand in the room which for Emily Dickinson was "freedom." The best bedroom in the house, a corner room, sunny, overlooking the main street of Amherst in front, the way to her brother Austin's house on the side. Here, at a small table with one drawer, she wrote most of her poems. Here she read Elizabeth Barrett's "Aurora Leigh," a woman poet's narrative poem of a woman poet's life; also George Eliot; Emerson; Carlyle; Shakespeare; Charlotte and Emily Brontë. Here I become, again, an insect, vibrating at the frames of windows, clinging to panes of glass, trying to connect. The scent here is very powerful. Here in this white-curtained, high-ceilinged room, a redhaired woman with hazel eyes and a contralto voice wrote poems about volcanoes, deserts, eternity, suicide, physical passion, wild beasts, rape, power, madness, separation, the daemon, the grave. Here, with a darning-needle, she bound these poems—heavily emended and often in variant versions—into booklets, secured with darning-thread, to be found and read after her death. Here she knew "freedom," listening from above-stairs to a visitor's piano-playing, escaping from the pantry where she was mistress of the household bread and puddings, watching, you feel, watching ceaselessly, the life of sober Main Street below. From this room she glided downstairs, her hand on the polished banister, to meet the complacent magazine editor, Thomas Higginson, unnerve him while claiming she herself was unnerved. "Your scholar," she signed herself in letters to him. But she was an independent scholar, used his criticism selectively, saw him rarely and always on *her* premises. It was a life deliberately organized on her terms. The terms she had been handed by society—Calvinist Protestantism, Romanticism, the nineteenth-century corseting of women's bodies, choices, and sexuality—could spell insanity to a woman genius. What this one had to do was retranslate her own unorthodox, subversive, sometimes volcanic propensities into a dialect called metaphor: her native language. "Tell all the Truth—but tell it Slant—." It is always what is under pressure in us, especially under pressure of concealment—that explodes in poetry.

The women and men in her life she equally converted into metaphor. The masculine pronoun in her poems can refer simultaneously to many aspects of the "masculine" in the patriarchal world—the god she engages in dialogue, again on *her* terms; her own creative powers, unsexing for a woman, the male power-figures in her immediate environment—the lawyer Edward Dickinson, her brother Austin, the preacher Wadsworth, the editor Bowles—it is far too limiting to trace that "He" to some specific lover, although that was the chief obsession of the legend-mongers for more than half a century. Obviously, Dickinson was attracted by and interested in men whose minds had something to offer her; she was, it is by now clear, equally attracted by and interested in women whose minds had something to offer her. There are many poems to and about women, and some which exist in two versions with alternate sets of pronouns. Her latest biographer, Richard Sewall, while rejecting an earlier Freudian biographer's theory that Dickinson was essentially a psycho-pathological case, the by-product of which happened to be poetry, does create a context in which the importance, and validity, of Dickinson's attachments to women may now, at last, be seen in full. She was always stirred by the existences of women like George Eliot or Elizabeth Barrett, who possessed strength of mind, articulateness, and energy. (She once characterized Elizabeth Fry and Florence Nightingale as "holy"—one suspects she merely meant, "great.")

But of course Dickinson's relationships with women were more than intellectual. They were deeply charged, and the sources both of passionate joy and pain. We are only beginning to be able to consider them in a social and historical context. The historian Carroll Smith-Rosenberg has shown that there was far less taboo on intense, even passionate and sensual, relationships between women in the American nineteenth-century "female world of love and ritual," as she terms it, than there was later in the twentieth century. Women expressed their attachments to other women both physically and verbally; a marriage did not dilute the strength of a female friendship, in which two women often shared the same bed during long visits, and wrote letters articulate with both physical and emotional longing. The nineteenth-century close woman friend, according to the many diaries and letters Smith-Rosenberg has studied, might be a far more important figure in a woman's life than the nineteenth-century husband. None of this was condemned as "lesbianism." We will understand Emily Dickinson better, read her poetry more perceptively, when the Freudian imputation of scandal and aberrance in women's love for women has been supplanted by a more informed, less misogynistic attitude toward women's experiences with each other.

But who, if you read through the seventeen hundred and seventy-five poems—who—woman or man—could have passed through that imagination and not come out transmuted? Given the space created by her in that corner room, with its window-light, its potted plants and work-table, given that personality, capable of imposing its terms on a household, on a whole community, what single theory could hope to contain her, when she'd put it all together in that space?

"Matty: here's freedom," I hear her saying as I speed back to Boston along Route 91, as I slip the turnpike ticket into the toll-collector's hand. I am thinking of a confined space in which the genius of the nineteenth-century female mind in America moved, inventing a language more varied, more compressed, more dense with implications, more complex of syntax, than any American poetic language to date; in the trail of that genius my mind has been moving, and with its language and images my mind still has to reckon, as the mind of a woman poet in America today.

In 1971 a postage stamp was issued in honor of Dickinson; the portrait derives from the one existing daguerreotype of her, with straight, center-parted hair, eyes staring somewhere beyond the camera, hands poised around a nosegay of flowers, in correct nineteenth-century style. On the first-day-of-issue envelope sent me by a friend there is, besides the postage stamp, an engraving of the poet as popular fancy has preferred her, in a white lace ruff and with hair as bouffant as if she had just stepped from a Boston beauty parlor. The poem chosen to represent her work to the American public is engraved, alongside a dew-gemmed rose, below the portrait:

If I can stop one heart from breaking
I shall not live in vain
If I can ease one life the aching
Or cool one pain
Or help one fainting robin
Unto his nest again
I shall not live in vain.

Now, this is extremely strange. It is a fact that in 1864 Emily Dickinson wrote this verse; and it is a verse which a hundred or more nineteenth-century versifiers could have written. In its undistinguished language, as in its conventional sentiment, it is remarkably untypical of the poet. Had she chosen to write many poems like this one we would have no "problem" of nonpublication, of editing, of estimating the poet at her true worth. Certainly the sentiment—a contented and unambiguous altruism—is one which even today might in some quarters be accepted as fitting from a female versifier—a kind of Girl Scout prayer. But we are talking about the woman who wrote:

> He fumbles at your Soul
> As Players at the Keys
> Before they drop full Music on—
> He stuns you by degrees—
> Prepares your brittle Nature
> For the Ethereal Blow
> By fainter Hammers—further heard—
> Then nearer—Then so slow
> Your breath has time to straighten—
> Your brain—to bubble Cool—
> Deals—One—Imperial—Thunderbolt—
> Then scalps your naked Soul—
>
> When winds take Forests in their Paws—
> The Universe—is still—
>
> (#315)

Much energy has been invested in trying to identify a concrete, flesh-and-blood male lover whom Dickinson is supposed to have renounced, and to the loss of whom can be traced the secret of her seclusion and the vein of much of her poetry. But the real question, given that the art of poetry is an art of transformation, is how this woman's mind and imagination may have used the masculine element in the world at large, or those elements personified as masculine—including the men she knew; how her relationship to this reveals itself in her images and language. In a patriarchal culture, specifically the Judeo-Christian, quasi-Puritan culture of nineteenth-century New England in which Dickinson grew up, still inflamed with religious revivals, and where the sermon was still an active, if perishing, literary form, the equation of divinity with maleness was so fundamental that it is hardly surprising to find Dickinson, like many an early mystic, blurring erotic with religious experience and imagery. The poem has intimations of both seduction and rape merged with the intense force of a religious experience. But are these metaphors for each other, or for something more intrinsic to Dickinson? Here is another:

He put the Belt around my life—
I heard the buckle snap—
And turned away, imperial,
My lifetime folding up—
Deliberate, as a Duke would do
A Kingdom's Title Deed
Henceforth, a Dedicated sort—
  Member of the Cloud.

Yet not too far to come at call—
And do the little Toils
That make the Circuit of the Rest—
And deal occasional smiles
To lives that stoop to notice mine—
And kindly ask it in—
Whose invitation, know you not
For Whom I must decline?

(#273)

These two poems are about possession, and they seem to me a poet's poems—that is, they are about the poet's relationship to her own power, which is exteriorized in masculine form, much as masculine poets have invoked the female Muse. In writing at all—particularly an unorthodox and original poetry like Dickinson's—women have often felt in danger of losing their status as women. And this status has always been defined in terms of relationship to men—as daughter, sister, bride, wife, mother, mistress, Muse. Since the most powerful figures in patriarchal culture have been men, it seems natural that Dickinson would assign a masculine gender to that in herself which did not fit in with the conventional ideology of womanliness. To recognize and acknowledge our own interior power has always been a path mined with risks for women; to acknowledge that power and commit oneself to it as Emily Dickinson did was an immense decision.

Most of us, unfortunately, have been exposed in the schoolroom to Dickinson's "little-girl" poems, her kittenish tones, as in "I'm Nobody! Who Are You?" (a poem whose underlying anger translates itself into archness) or

I hope the Father in the skies
Will lift his little girl—
Old fashioned—naughty—everything
Over the stile of "Pearl."

(#70)

or the poems about bees and robins. One critic—Richard Chase—has noted that in the nineteenth century "one of the careers open to women was perpetual childhood." A strain in Dickinson's letters and some—though by far a minority—of her poems was a self-diminutization, almost as if to offset and deny—or even disguise—her actual dimensions as she must have experienced them. And this emphasis on her own "littleness," along with the deliberate strangeness of her tactics of seclusion, have been, until recently, accepted as the prevailing character of the poet: the fragile poetess in white, sending flowers and poems by messenger to unseen friends, letting down baskets of gingerbread to the neighborhood children from her bedroom window; writing, but somehow naively. John Crowe Ransom, arguing for the editing and standardization of Dickinson's punctuation and typography, calls her "a little home-keeping person" who, "while she had a proper notion of the final destiny of her poems ... was not one of those poets who had advanced to that later stage of operations where manuscripts are prepared for the printer, and the poet's diction has to make concessions to the publisher's style-book." (In short, Emily Dickinson did not wholly know her trade, and Ransom believes a "publisher's style-book" to have the last word on poetic diction.) He goes on to print several of her poems, altered by him "with all possible forbearance." What might, in a male writer—a Thoreau, let us say, or a Christopher Smart or William Blake—seem a legitimate strangeness, a unique intention, has been in one of our two major poets devalued into a kind of naiveté, girlish ignorance, feminine lack of professionalism, just as the poet herself has been made into a sentimental object. ("Most of us are half in love with this dead girl," confesses Archibald Mac-Leish. Dickinson was fifty-five when she died.)

It is true that more recent critics, including her most recent biographer, have gradually begun to approach the poet in terms of her greatness rather than her littleness, the decisiveness of her choices instead of the surface oddities of her life or the romantic crises of her legend. But unfortunately anthologists continue to plagiarize other anthologies, to reprint her in edited, even bowdlerized versions; the popular image of her and of her works lags behind the changing consciousness of scholars and specialists. There still does not exist a selection from her poems which depicts her in her fullest range. Dickinson's greatness cannot be measured in terms of twenty-five or fifty or even five-hundred "perfect" lyrics; it has to be seen as the accumulation it is. Poets, even, are not always fully acquainted with the full dimensions of her work, or the sense one gets, reading in the one-volume complete edition (let alone the three-volume variorum edition) of a mind engaged in a lifetime's musing on essential problems of language, identity, separation, relationship, the integrity of the self; a mind capable of describing psychological states more accurately than any poet except Shakespeare. I have been surprised at how narrowly her work, still, is known by women who are writing poetry, how much her legend has gotten in the way of her being re-possessed, as a source and a foremother.

I know that for me, reading her poems as a child and then as a young girl already seriously writing poetry, she was a problematic figure. I first read her in the selection heavily edited by her niece which appeared in 1937; a later and fuller edition appeared in 1945 when I was sixteen, and the complete, unbowdlerized edition by Johnson did not appear until fifteen years later. The publication of each of these editions was crucial to me in successive decades of my life. More than any other poet, Emily Dickinson seemed to tell me that the intense inner event, the personal and psychological, was inseparable from the universal; that there was a range for psychological poetry beyond mere self expression. Yet the legend of the life was troubling, because it seemed to whisper that a woman who undertook such explorations must pay with renunciation, isolation, and incorporeality. With the publication of the *Complete Poems*, the legend seemed to recede into unimportance beside the unquestionable power and importance of the mind revealed there. But taking possession of Emily Dickinson is still no simple matter.

The 1945 edition, entitled *Bolts of Melody*, took its title from a poem which struck me at the age of sixteen and which still, thirty years later, arrests my imagination:

I would not paint—a picture—
I'd rather be the One
Its bright impossibility

To dwell—delicious—on—
And wonder how the fingers feel
Whose rare—celestial—stir
Evokes so sweet a Torment—
Such sumptuous—Despair—

I would not talk, like Cornets—
I'd rather be the One
Raised softly to the Ceilings—
And out, and easy on—
Through the Villages of Ether
Myself endured Balloon
By but a lip of Metal
The pier to my Pontoon—

Nor would I be a Poet—
It's finer—own the Ear—
Enamored—impotent—content
The License to revere,
A privilege so awful
What would the Dower be,
Had I the Art to stun myself
With Bolts of Melody!

(#505)

This poem is about choosing an orthodox "feminine" role: the receptive rather than the creative; the viewer rather than the painter; listener rather than musician; acted-upon rather than active. Yet even while ostensibly choosing this role she wonders "how the fingers feel / Whose rare—celestial –stir / Evokes so sweet a Torment—" and the "feminine" role is praised in a curious sequence of adjectives: "Enamored—*impotent*—content—." The strange paradox of this poem—its exquisite irony—is that it is about choosing not to be a poet, a poem which is gainsaid by no fewer than one thousand seven hundred and seventy-five poems made during the writer's life, including itself. Moreover, the images of the poem rise to a climax (like the Balloon she evokes) but the climax happens as she describes, not what it is to be the receiver, but the maker and receiver at once: "A privilege so awful / What would the Dower be / Had I the Art to stun myself / With Bolts of Melody!"—a climax which recalls the poem: "He fumbles at your soul / As Players at the Keys / Before they drop full Music on—." And of course, in writing those lines she possesses herself of that privilege and that "dower." I have said that this is a poem of exquisite ironies. It is, indeed, though in a very different mode, related to Dickinson's "little-girl" strategy. The woman who feels herself to be Vesuvius at home has need of a mask, at least, of innocuousness and of containment.

> On my volcano grows the Grass
> A meditative spot—
> An acre for a Bird to choose
> Would be the General thought—
>
> How red the Fire rocks below—
> How insecure the sod
> Did I disclose
> Would populate with awe my solitude.
>
> (#1677)

Power, even masked, can still be perceived as destructive.

> A still—Volcano—Life—
> That flickered in the night—
> When it was dark enough to do
> Without erasing sight—
>
> A quiet—Earthquake style—
> Too subtle to suspect
> By natures this side Naples—
> The North cannot detect
>
> The Solemn—Torrid—Symbol—
> The lips that never lie—
> Whose hissing Corals part—and shut—
> And Cities—ooze away—
>
> (#601)

Dickinson's biographer and editor Thomas Johnson has said that she often felt herself possessed by a demonic force, particularly in the year

1862 when she was writing at the height of her drive. There are many poems besides "He put the Belt around my Life" which could be read as poems of possession by the daemon—poems which can also be, and have been, read, as poems of possessions by the deity, or by a human lover. I suggest that a woman's poetry about her relationship to her daemon—her own active, creative power—has in patriarchal culture used the language of heterosexual love or patriarchal theology. Ted Hughes tells us that

> The eruption of (Dickinson's) imagination and poetry followed when she shifted her passion, with the energy of desperation, from (the) lost man onto his only possible substitute, —the Universe in its Divine aspect ... Thereafter, the marriage that had been denied in the real world, went forward in the spiritual ... just as the Universe in its Divine aspect became the mirror-image of her "husband," so the whole religious dilemma of New England, at that most critical moment in its history, became the mirror-image of her relationship to him, of her "marriage" in fact.

This seems to me to miss the point on a grand scale. There are facts we need to look at. First, Emily Dickinson did not marry. And her non-marrying was neither a pathological retreat as John Cody sees it, nor probably even a conscious decision; it was a fact in her life as in her contemporary Christina Rossetti's; both women had more primary needs. Second: unlike Rossetti, Dickinson did not become a religiously dedicated woman; she was heretical, heterodox, in her religious opinions, and stayed away from church and dogma. What, in fact, did she allow to "put the Belt around her Life"—what *did* wholly occupy her mature years and possess her? For "Whom" did she decline the invitations of other lives? The writing of poetry. Nearly two thousand poems. Three hundred and sixty-five poems in the year of her fullest power. What was it like to be writing poetry you knew (and I am sure she did know) was of a class by itself—to be fueled by the energy it took first to confront, then to copy out the poems and lay them in a trunk, or send a few here and there to friends or relatives as occasional verse or as gestures of confidence? I am sure she knew who she was, as she indicates in this poem:

Myself was formed—a carpenter—
An unpretending time
My Plane—and I, together wrought
Before a Builder came—

To measure our attainments
Had we the Art of Boards
Sufficiently developed—He'd hire us
At Halves—

My Tools took Human—Faces—
The Bench, where we had toiled—
Against the Man—persuaded—
We—Temples Build—I said—
(#488)

This is a poem of the great year 1862, the year in which she first sent a few poems to Thomas Higginson for criticism. Whether it antedates or postdates that occasion is unimportant; it is a poem of knowing one's measure, regardless of the judgments of others.

There are many poems which carry the weight of this knowledge. Here is another one:

I'm ceded—I've stopped being Theirs—
The name They dropped upon my face
With water, in the country church
Is finished using, now,
And They can put it with my dolls,
My childhood, and the string of spools,
I've finished threading—too—

Baptized before, without the choice,
But this time, consciously, of Grace—
Unto supremest name—
Called to my Fill—the Crescent dropped—
Existence's whole Arc, filled up
With one small Diadem.

My second Rank—too small the first—
Crowned—Crowing—on my Father's breast—
A half unconscious Queen—
But this time—Adequate—Erect—
With Will to choose—or to reject—
And I choose—just a Crown—
(#508)

Now, this poem partakes of the imagery of being "twice-born" or, in Christian liturgy, "confirmed"—and if this poem had been written by Christina Rossetti I would be inclined to give more weight to a theological reading. But it was written by Emily Dickinson, who used the Christian metaphor far more than she let it use her. This is a poem of great pride—not pridefulness, but *self*-confirmation—and it is curious how little Dickinson's critics, perhaps misled by her diminutives, have recognized the will and pride in her poetry. It is a poem of movement from childhood to womanhood, of transcending the patriarchal condition of bearing her father's name and "Crowing—on my Father's breast—." She is now a conscious Queen, "Adequate—Erect? With Will to choose—or to reject—."

There is one poem which is the real "onlie begetter" of my thoughts here about Dickinson; a poem I have mused over, repeated to myself, taken into myself over many years. I think it is a poem about possession by the daemon, about the dangers and risks of such possession if you are a woman, about the knowledge that power in a woman can seem destructive, and that you cannot live without the daemon once it has possessed you. The archetype of the daemon as masculine is beginning to change, but it has been real for women up until now. But this woman poet also perceives herself as lethal weapon:

My life had stood—a Loaded Gun—
In Corners—till a Day
The Owner passed—identified—
And carried me away—

And now We roam in Sovereign Woods—
And now We hunt the Doe—
And every time I speak for Him—
The Mountains straight reply—

And do I smile, such cordial light
Upon the Valley glow—
It is as a Vesuvian face
Had let its pleasure through—

And when at Night—our good Day done—
I guard My Master's Head—
"Tis better than the Eider-Duck's
Deep Pillow—to have shared—

To foe of His—I'm deadly foe—
None stir the second time—
On whom I lay a Yellow Eye—
Or an emphatic Thumb—

Though I than he –may longer live
He longer must—than I—
For I have but the power to kill,
Without—the power to die—
(#754)

Here the poet sees herself as split, not between anything so simple as "masculine" and "feminine" identity but between the hunter, admittedly masculine, but also a human person, an active, willing being, and the gun—an object, condemned to remain inactive until the hunter—the *owner*—takes possession of it. The gun contains an energy capable of rousing echoes in the mountains and lighting up the valleys; it is also deadly, "Vesuvian"; it is also its owner's defender against the "foe." It is the gun, furthermore, who *speaks for him.* If there is a female consciousness in this poem it is buried deeper than the images: it exists in the ambivalence toward power, which is extreme. Active willing and creation in women are forms of aggression, and aggression is both "the power to kill" and punishable by death. The union of gun with hunter embodies the danger of identifying and taking hold of her forces, not least that in so doing she risks defining herself—and being defined as aggressive, as unwomanly ("and now we hunt the Doe"), and as potentially lethal. That which she experiences in herself as energy and potency can also be experienced as pure destruction. The final stanza, with its precarious balance of phrasing, seems a desperate attempt to resolve the ambivalence; but, I think, it is no resolution, only a further extension of ambivalence.

> Though I than he—may longer live
> He longer must—than I—
> For I have but the power to kill,
> Without—the power to die—

The poet experiences herself as loaded gun, imperious energy; yet without the Owner, the possessor, she is merely lethal. Should that possession abandon her—but the thought is unthinkable: "He longer *must* than I." The pronoun is masculine; the antecedent is what Keats called "The Genius of Poetry."

I do not pretend to have—I don't even wish to have—explained this poem, accounted for its every image; it will reverberate with new tones long after my words about it have ceased to matter. But I think that for us, at this time, it is a central poem in understanding Emily Dickinson, and ourselves, and the condition of the woman artist, particularly in the nineteenth century. It seems likely that the nineteenth-century woman poet, especially, felt the medium of poetry as dangerous, in ways that the woman novelist did not feel the medium of fiction to be. In writing even such a novel of elemental sexuality and anger as *Wuthering Heights*, Emily Brontë could at least theoretically separate herself from her characters; they were, after all, fictitious beings. Moreover, the novel is or can be a construct, planned and organized to deal with human experiences on one level at a time. Poetry is too much rooted in the unconscious; it presses too close against the barriers of repression; and the nineteenth-century woman had much to repress. It is interesting that Elizabeth Barrett tried to fuse poetry and fiction in writing "Aurora Leigh"—perhaps apprehending the need for fictional characters to carry the charge of her experience as a woman artist. But with the exception of "Aurora Leigh" and Christina Rossetti's "Goblin Market"*—that extraordinary and little-known poem drenched in oral eroticism—Emily Dickinson's is the only poetry in English by a woman of that century which pierces so far beyond the ideology of the "feminine" and the conventions of womanly feeling. To write it at all, she had to be willing to enter chambers of the self in which

Ourself behind ourself, concealed—
Should startle most—

and to relinquish control there, to take those risks, she had to create a relationship to the outer world where she could feel in control.

It is an extremely painful and dangerous way to live—split between a publicly acceptable persona and a part of yourself that you perceive as the essential, the creative and powerful self, yet also as possibly unacceptable, perhaps even monstrous.

Much Madness is divinest sense—
To a discerning Eye—
Much sense—the starkest Madness.
'Tis the Majority
In this, as All, prevail—
Assent—and you are sane—
Demur—you're straightway dangerous—
And handled with a chain—

(#435)

For many women the stresses of this splitting have led, in a world so ready to assert our innate passivity and to deny our independence and creativity, to extreme consequences: the mental asylum, self-imposed silence, recurrent depression, suicide, and often severe loneliness.

Dickinson is *the* American poet whose work consisted in exploring states of psychic extremity. For a long time, as we have seen, this fact was obscured by the kinds of selections made from her work by timid if well-meaning editors. In fact, Dickinson was a great psychologist; and like every great psychologist, she began with the material she had at hand: herself. She had to possess the courage to enter, through language, states which most people deny or veil with silence.

The first Day's Night had come—
And grateful that a thing
So terrible—had been endured—
I told my soul to sing—

She said her Strings were snapt—
Her Bow—to Atoms blown—

And so to mend her—gave me work
Until another Morn—

And then—a Day as huge
As Yesterdays in pairs,
Unrolled its horror in my face—

My Brain—begun to laugh—
I mumbled—like a fool—
And tho' 'tis years ago—that Day—
My brain keeps giggling—still.

And Something's odd—within—
That person that I was—
And this One—do not feel the same—
Could it be Madness—this?

(#410)

Dickinson's letters acknowledge a period of peculiarly intense personal crisis; her biographers have variously ascribed it to the pangs of renunciation of an impossible love, or to psychic damage deriving from her mother's presumed depression and withdrawal after her birth. What concerns us here is the fact that she chose to probe the nature of this experience in language:

The Soul has Bandaged moments—
When too appalled to stir—
She feels some ghastly Fright come up
And stop to look at her—

Salute her—with long fingers—
Caress her freezing hair—
Sip, Goblin, from the very lips
The Lover—hovered—o'er—
Unworthy, that a thought so mean
Accost a Theme—so—fair—

The soul has moments of Escape—
When bursting all the doors—

She dances like a Bomb, abroad,
And swings upon the hours …

The Soul's retaken moments—
When, Felon led along,
With shackles on the plumed feet,
And staples, in the Song,

The Horror welcomes her, again,
These, are not brayed of Tongue—

(#512)

In this poem, the word "Bomb" is dropped, almost carelessly, as a correlative for the soul's active, liberated states—it occurs in a context of apparent euphoria, but its implications are more than euphoric—they are explosive, destructive. The "Horror" from which in such moments the soul escapes has a masculine, "goblin" form, and suggests the perverse and terrifying rape of a "bandaged" and powerless self. In at least one poem, Dickinson depicts the actual process of suicide:

He scanned it—staggered—
Dropped the Loop
To Past or Period—
Caught helpless at a sense as if
His mind were going blind—
Groped up—to see if God was there—
Groped backward at Himself—
Caressed a Trigger absently
And wandered out of Life.

(#1062)

The precision of knowledge in this brief poem is such that we must assume that Dickinson had, at least in fantasy, drifted close to that state in which the "Loop" that binds us to "Past or Period" is "dropped" and we grope randomly at what remains of abstract notions of sense, God, or self, before—almost absent-mindedly—reaching for a solution. But it's worth noting that this is a poem in which the suicidal experience has been distanced, refined, transformed through a devastating accuracy of language. It is not suicide that is studied here, but the dissociation of self and mind and world which precedes.

Dickinson was convinced that a life worth living could be found within the mind and against the grain of external circumstance: "Reverse cannot befall/That fine prosperity/Whose Sources are interior—" (#395). The horror, for her, was that which set "Staples in the Song"—the numbing and freezing of the interior, a state she describes over and over:

> There is a Languor of the Life
> More imminent than Pain—
> 'Tis Pain's Successor—When the Soul
> Has suffered all it can—
>
> A Drowsiness—diffuses—
> A Dimness like a Fog
> Envelopes Consciousness—
> As Mists—obliterate a Crag.
>
> The Surgeon—does not blanch—at pain
> His Habit—is severe—
> But tell him that it ceased to feel—
> That creature lying there—
>
> And he will tell you—skill is late—
> A Mightier than He—
> Has ministered before Him—
> There's no Vitality.
>
> (#396)

I think the equation surgeon-artist is a fair one here; the artist can work with the materials of pain; she cuts to probe and heal; but she is powerless at the point where

> After great pain, a formal feeling comes—
> The nerves sit ceremonious, like Tombs—
> The stiff Heart questions was it He, that bore,
> And Yesterday, or Centuries before?

The Feet, mechanical, go round—
Of Ground, or Air, or Ought—
A Wooden way
Regardless grown,
A Quartz contentment, like a stone—

This is the Hour of Lead
Remembered, if outlived
As Freezing persons, recollect the Snow—
First—Chill—then Stupor—then the letting go—
(#341)

For the poet, the terror is precisely in those periods of psychic death, when even the possibility of work is negated; her "occupation's gone." Yet she also describes the unavailing effort to numb emotion:

Me from Myself—to banish—
Had I Art—
Impregnable my Fortress
Unto All Heart—

But since Myself—assault Me—
How have I peace
Except by subjugating
Consciousness?

And since We're mutual Monarch
How this be
Except by Abdication—
Me—of Me?
(#642)

The possibility of abdicating oneself—of ceasing to be—remains.

Severe Service of myself
I—hastened to demand
To fill the awful longitude
Your life had left behind—

I worried Nature with my Wheels
When Hers had ceased to run—
When she had put away her Work
My own had just begun.

I strove to weary Brain and Bone—
To harass to fatigue
The glittering Retinue of nerves—
Vitality to clog

To some dull comfort Those obtain
Who put a Head away
They knew the Hair to—
And forget the color of the Day—

Affliction would not be appeased—
The Darkness braced as firm
As all my strategem had been
The Midnight to confirm—

No drug for Consciousness—can be—
Alternative to die
Is Nature's only Pharmacy
For Being's Malady—

(#786)

Yet consciousness—not simply the capacity to suffer, but the capacity to experience intensely at every instant—creates of death not a blotting-out but a final illumination:

This Consciousness that is aware
Of Neighbors and the Sun
Will be the one aware of Death
And that itself alone

Is traversing the interval
Experience between
And most profound experiment
Appointed unto Men—

How adequate unto itself
Its properties shall be
Itself unto itself and none
Shall make discovery.

Adventure most unto itself
The Soul condemned to be—
Attended by a single Hound
Its own identity.

(#822)

The poet's relationship to her poetry has, it seems to me—and I am not speaking only of Emily Dickinson—a twofold nature. Poetic language—the poem on paper—is a concretization of the poetry of the world at large, the self, and the forces within the self; and those forces are rescued from formlessness, lucidified, and integrated in the act of writing poems. But there is a more ancient concept of the poet, which is that she is endowed to speak for those who do not have the gift of language, or to see for those who—for whatever reasons—are less conscious of what they are living through. It is as though the risks of the poet's existence can be put to some use beyond her own survival.

The Province of the Saved
Should be the Art—To save—
Through Skill obtained in themselves—
The Science of the Grave

No Man can understand
But He that hath endured
The Dissolution—in Himself—
That man—be qualified

To qualify Despair
To Those who failing new—
Mistake Defeat for Death—Each time—
Till acclimated—to—

(#539)

The poetry of extreme states, the poetry of danger, can allow its readers to go further in our own awareness, take risks we might not have dared; it says, at least: "Someone has been here before."

> The Soul's distinct Connection
> With immortality
> Is best disclosed by Danger
> Or quick Calamity—
>
> As Lightning on a Landscape
> Exhibits Sheets of Place—
> Not yet suspected—but for Flash—
> And Click—and Suddenness.
>
> (#974)

> Crumbling is not an instant's Act
> A fundamental pause
> Dilapidation's processes
> Are organized Decays.
>
> 'Tis first a cobweb on the Soul
> A Cuticle of Dust
> A Borer in the Axis
> An Elemental Rust—
>
> Ruin is formal—Devil's work
> Consecutive and slow—
> Fail in an instant—no man did
> Slipping—is Crash's law.
>
> (#997)

> I felt a Cleaving in my Mind
> As if my Brain had split—
> I tried to match it—Seam by Seam—
> But could not make them fit.
>
> The thought behind, I strove to join
> Unto the thought before—

But Sequence ravelled out of Sound
Like Balls—upon a Floor.

(#937)

There are many more Emily Dickinsons than I have tried to call up here. Wherever you take hold of her, she proliferates. I wish I had time here to explore her complex sense of Truth; to follow the thread we unravel when we look at the numerous and passionate poems she wrote to or about women; to probe her ambivalent feelings about fame, a subject pursued by many male poets before her; simply to examine the poems in which she is directly apprehending the natural world. No one since the seventeenth century had reflected more variously or more probingly upon death and dying. What I have tried to do here is follow through some of the origins and consequences of her choice to be, not only a poet but a woman who explored her own mind, without any of the guidelines of orthodoxy. To say "yes" to her powers was not simply a major act of nonconformity in the nineteenth century; even in our own time it has been assumed that Emily Dickinson, not patriarchal society, was "the problem." The more we come to recognize the unwritten and written laws and taboos underpinning patriarchy, the less problematical, surely, will seem the methods she chose.

ALLEN TATE

New England Culture and Emily Dickinson

I

The work of a great poet needs no special features of difficulty to make it mysterious. When it has them, the reputation of the poet is likely to remain ambiguous. This is still true of Donne, and it is true of Emily Dickinson, whose verse appeared in an age unfavorable for the exercise of intelligence in poetry. Her poetry is not like any other poetry of her time; it is not like any of the innumerable styles of verse written today. In still another respect it is far removed from us. It is a poetry of ideas, and it demands of the reader a point of view—not an opinion of Prohibition or of the League of Nations, but an ingrained philosophy that is more fundamental, the kind of settled attitude that is almost extinct in this eclectic age. Yet it is not the sort of poetry of ideas which, like Pope's, requires a point of view only. It requires also, for the deepest understanding, which must go beneath the verbal excitement of her style, a highly developed sense of the specific quality of poetry—a quality that most persons accept incidentally as the by-product of something else that the poet thinks he has to say. This is one reason why Miss Dickinson's poetry has not been widely read.

There is another reason, and it is intimately involved with the problem peculiar to a poetry that comes out of fundamental ideas. We

---

From *The Symposium*, pp. 206-26, 1932. Reprinted with permission of the Helen Dwight Reid Educational Foundation. Published by Heldref Publications, 1319 Eighteenth St., NW, Washington, DC 20036-1802.

lack a tradition of criticism. There are no points of critical reference that were passed to us from a preceding generation. I am not praising here the so-called dead-hand of tradition, but rather a rational insight into the meaning of the present in terms of some imaginable past implicit in our own lives; we need a body of ideas that can bear upon the course of the spirit and yet remain fixed as a rational instrument. We ignore the present, which is momently translated into a past, and derive our standards from imaginative constructions of the future. Contingency invariably breaks these down, leaving us the intellectual chaos which is the sore distress of modern criticism.

Still another fact stands between us and Miss Dickinson. It is the failure of the scholars to feel any curiosity about her. We have an institutionalized scholarship, but that is no substitute for a critical tradition. Miss Dickinson's value to the research scholar, who likes historical difficulty for its own sake, is slight; she is too near to possess the remoteness of literature. Perhaps her appropriate setting would be the age of Cowley or of Donne. Yet in her own historical setting she is, nevertheless, remarkable and special.

Even more than Hawthorne she is a special case of nineteenth century puritanism. The intellectual climate into which she was born, in 1830, had, as all times have, the features of a transition, but the period was a major crisis culminating in the War between the States. After that war, in New England as well as in the South, the crises were definitely minor until the Great War. It is certainly bad history to assume that the surrender of Cornwallis in 1781 freed America from the domination of Europe: the War between the States was the second and decisive struggle of what one may call the western spirit, against the European, and this western spirit won. The chief forces of European history since the Middle Ages were concentrated in the war between the North and the South. The South had some characteristics all its own, such as the negro and a landed democracy, but there, nevertheless, the most conservative of the European orders had with great power come back to life. In the North, opposing the Southern feudalism, had grown up a strong industrial society which was and still is 'forward-looking'; it contained all the middle-class urban impulses that have been hostile to the agrarian classes of Europe since the Reformation. The transformation of Europe, in Europe itself, has been gradual. The transformation of Europe, in America, was—because its two spiritual poles were situated here—sudden and dramatic.

Yet in New England, a generation before the war of 1861–65, the issue had been met. When Samuel Slater in 1790 thwarted the British embargo on mill-machinery by committing to memory the whole design of a cotton spinner and bringing it to Massachusetts, he planted the seed of the 'western spirit.' By 1825 its growth in the east was rank enough to begin choking out the ideas and habits of living that New England along with Virginia had kept in unconscious allegiance to Europe. To the casual observer, perhaps, the New England character of 1830 was largely an eighteenth-century character. But the theocracy was on the decline, and industrialism was rising fast—as Emerson, in an unusually lucid moment put it, things are in the saddle; and the energy that built the meeting-house ran the factory.

Now the idea that moved the theocratic state is the most interesting historically of all American ideas. It was, of course, powerful in seventeenth-century England, but in America, where the long arm of Laud could not reach, it acquired an unchecked social and political influence. The important thing to remember about the puritan theocracy is that it permeated, as it could never have done in England, a whole society. It gave a final, definite meaning to life, the life of pious and impious, of learned and vulgar alike. It gave—and this is its significance for the work of Emily Dickinson, and in only slightly lesser degree for the work of Melville and Hawthorne—it gave an heroic proportion and a tragic mode to the experience of the individual. The history of the New England theocracy, from Apostle Eliot to Cotton Mather, is rich in gigantic intellects that broke down—or so it must appear to an outsider—in a kind of moral decadence and depravity. Socially we may not like the New England idea. It had an immense, incalculable value for literature: it dramatized the human soul. It created the perfect 'literary situation'—a situation that the Southern culture did not, or never had enough time, to produce.

But after 1830 the great fortunes were made (in the rum, slave, and milling industries), and New England became a museum. The whatnots groaned under the load of knick-knacks, the fine china dogs and cats, the pieces of Oriental jade, the chips off the leaning tower at Pisa. There were the rare books and the cosmopolitan learning. It was all about equally displayed as the evidence of a superior culture; for the Gilded Age had already begun. But culture, in the true sense, was disappearing. Where the old order, formidable as it was, had held all this personal experience, this eclectic excitement, in a comprehensible whole, the new order tended to flatten it out in a common experience that was not quite in common; it exalted more and more the personal and the unique in the interior sense. Where the old-fashioned puritans got together on a rigid doctrine, and could thus be individualists in conduct, the nineteenth-century New Englander, lacking a genuine cultural center, began to be a social conformist. The common idea of the Redemption, for example, was replaced by the conformist idea of respectability among neighbors whose spiritual disorder, not very evident at the surface, was becoming acute. A great idea was breaking up, and society moved towards an external uniformity which is usually the measure of the spiritual chaos inside.

At this juncture Emerson came upon the scene; the Lucifer of Concord, he had better be called hereafter, for he was the light-bearer who could see nothing but light, and was fearfully blind. He looked around and saw the uniformity of life, and called it the dead-hand of tradition, the tyranny of the theological idea. The death of Priam put an end to the hope of Troy, but it was a slight feat of arms for the doughty Pyrrhus; Priam was an old gentleman and almost dead. So was the theocracy; and Emerson killed it. In this way he accelerated a tendency that he disliked. It was a great intellectual mistake. By it Emerson unwittingly became the prophet of a piratical industrialism, a consequence of his own wordy individualism that he could not foresee. He hoisted himself on his own petard.

He destroyed more than any other man the puritan drama of the soul. The age that followed, from 1865 on, was a genteel secularism, a mildly didactic order of feeling whose ornaments were Lowell, Longfellow and Holmes. "After Emerson had done his work," says Mr. Robert Penn Warren, "any tragic possibilities in that culture were dissipated." Hawthorne alone in his time kept pure, in the primitive terms, the primitive vision; he brings the puritan tragedy to its climax. Man, measured by a great idea outside himself, is found wanting. But in Emerson man is greater than any idea, and being himself the Over-Soul is potentially perfect; there is no struggle because—I state the Emersonian doctrine, which is very slippery, in its extreme terms—because there is no possibility of error. There is no drama in human character because there is no tragic fault. It is not surprising, then, that after Emerson New England literature tastes like a drink of Cambric tea. Its very center has disappeared. There is Hawthorne looking back, there is Emerson looking not too clearly at anything ahead: Emily Dickinson, who has in her something of them both, comes in somewhere between.

With the exception of Poe there is no American poet whose work so steadily emerges, under pressure of certain disintegrating obsessions, from the framework of moral character. There is none of whom it is truer to say that the poet *is* the poetry. Perhaps this explains the zeal that her admirers feel for her biography; it explains, in part at least, the gratuitous mystery that Mrs. Bianchi, a niece of the poet and the official biographer, makes of her life. The devoted controversy that Miss Josephine Pollitt and Miss Genevieve Taggard have started with their excellent books shows the extent to which the critics feel the intimate connection of her life and work. Admiration and affection are pleased to linger over the details of a great life, but the solution to the Dickinson enigma is peculiarly superior to fact.

The meaning of the identity—which we merely feel—of character and poetry would be exceedingly obscure, even if we could draw up a kind of Binet correlation between the two sets of facts. She was a recluse; but her poetry is rich in a profound and varied experience. Where did she get it? Now some of the biographers, nervous in the presence of this discrepancy, are eager to find her a love affair, and I think this search is due to a modern prejudice to the effect that no virgin can know enough to write poetry. We shall never learn where she got the rich quality of her mind. The moral image that we have of Miss Dickinson stands out in every poem; it is that of a dominating spinster whose very sweetness must have been terrible. Yet her poetry constantly moves within an absolute order of truths that overwhelmed her simply because to her they were unalterably fixed. It is dangerous to assume that her 'life,' which to the biographers means the thwarted love-affair she is supposed to have had, gave to her poetry a decisive direction. It is even more dangerous to suppose that it made her a poet.

Poetry is mysterious, but a poet when all is said is not much more mysterious than a banker. The critics remain spellbound by the technical license of her verse and by the puzzle of her personal life. Personality is always a legitimate interest because it is incurable, but as a personal interest only; it will never give up the key to any one's verse. Used to that end, the interest is false. "It is apparent," writes Mr. Conrad Aiken, "that Miss Dickinson became a hermit by deliberate and conscious choice"—a sensible remark that we cannot repeat too often. If it were necessary to explain her seclusion with disappointment in love, there would remain the discrepancy between what the seclusion produced and what brought it about. The effect, which is her poetry, would too easily exhaust the simple cause. For this cause would reach into the whole complex of anterior fact, which was the social and religious structure of New England.

The problem to be kept in mind is thus the meaning of her 'deliberate and conscious' decision to withdraw from life to her upstairs room. This simple fact is not very important. But that it must have been her only way of acting out her part in the history of her culture, which made, with the variations of circumstance, a single demand upon all its representatives—this is of the greatest consequence. All pity for Miss Dickinson's 'starved life' is misdirected. Her life was one of the richest and deepest ever lived on this continent.

When she went upstairs and closed the door, she mastered life by rejecting it. Others in their way had done it before; still others did it later. If we suppose—which is to suppose the improbable—that the love-affair precipitated the seclusion, it was only a pretext; she would have found another. (All accounts agree that her lover, whoever he was, was a married man—for her purposes, not an accident.) Mastery of the world by rejecting the world is the doctrine, even if it was not always the practice, of Jonathan Edwards and Cotton Mather. It is the meaning of fate in Hawthorne: his people are fated to withdraw from the world and to be destroyed. And it is the exclusive theme of Henry James.

There is a moral emphasis that connects Hawthorne, James, and Miss Dickinson, and I think it is instructive. Between Hawthorne and James lies an epoch. The temptation to sin, in Hawthorne, is, in James, transformed into the temptation not to do the 'decent thing.' A whole world-scheme, a complete cosmic background, has shrunk to the dimensions of the individual conscience. This epoch between Hawthorne and James lies in Emerson. James found himself in the post-Emersonian world, and he could not, without violating the detachment proper to an artist, undo Emerson's work; he had that kind of intelligence which refuses to break its head against history. There was left to him only the value, the historic role, of rejection. He could merely escape from the physical presence of that world which, for convenience, we may call Emerson's world; he could only take his Americans to Europe upon the vain quest of something that they had lost at home. His characters, fleeing the wreckage of the puritan culture, preserved only their honor. Honor became a sort of forlorn hope struggling against the forces of 'pure fact' that got loose in the middle of the century. Honor alone is a poor weapon against nature, being too personal, finical, and proud, and James achieved a victory only by refusing to engage the whole force of the enemy.

In Emily Dickinson the conflict takes place on a vaster field. Now the enemy to all those New Englanders was Nature, and Miss Dickinson saw into the character of this enemy more deeply than any of the others. The general symbol for her is Death, and her weapon against Death is the entire powerful dumb-show of the puritan mythology led by Redemption and Immortality. Morally speaking, the problem for James and Miss Dickinson is similar. But her advantages were greater than his: they lay in the availability to her of the puritan ideas on the theological plane.

These ideas are, in her poetry, being momently assailed by the disintegrating force of Nature (appearing as Death) which, although it constantly breaks them down, constantly redefines and strengthens them. The values are purified by the triumphant immersion in Nature, by their power to recover from Nature. The poet attains to a mastery over experience by facing its utmost implications. There is the clash of powerful opposites, and in all great poetry—for Emily Dickinson is a great poet—it issues in a stasis of abstraction and sensation in which the two elements may be, of course, distinguished logically, but not really. We are shown our roots in nature by examining our differences with nature; we are renewed by nature without being delivered into her hands. When it is possible for a poet to perform this task with the greatest imaginative comprehension, a possibility that the poet cannot himself create, we have the perfect literary situation. Only a few times in the history of English poetry has this situation come about. Dante, of course, had it preëminently, but in England it lies in the period between about 1580 and the Restoration. There was a similar age in New England from which emerged two talents of the first order—Hawthorne and Emily Dickinson.

If there is an epoch between James and Miss Dickinson, between her and Hawthorne there exists a difference of intellectual quality. She lacks almost radically the power to seize upon and understand abstractions for their own sake; she does not separate them from the sense perception that she is so marvellously adept at; like Donne, she *perceives abstraction* and *thinks sensation*. But Hawthorne was a master of ideas, within a limited range; this narrowness limited him to his own kind of life, his own society, and out of it grew his typical forms of experience, his steady, almost obsessed vision of man; it explains his depth and intensity. Yet he is always conscious of the abstract, doctrinal aspect of his mind, and when his vision of action and emotion is weak, his work becomes didactic. Now Miss Dickinson's poetry often runs in a quasi-homiletic form, but it is never didactic. Her very ignorance, her lack of formal intellectual training, spared her the risk that imperiled Hawthorne. She cannot reason at all. She can only *see*. It is impossible to imagine what she might have done with drama or fiction, for not approaching the puritan temper, and through it the puritan myth, through human action, she is able to grasp the terms of the myth directly and by a feat that amounts almost to anthropomorphism, to give them a luminous tension, a kind of drama, among themselves.

One of the perfect poems in English is *The Chariot*, and it exemplifies better than anything else she wrote the special quality of her mind; I think it will illuminate the tendency of this discussion:

Because I could not stop for death,
He kindly stopped for me;
The carriage held but just ourselves
And immortality.

We slowly drove, he knew no haste,
And I had put away
My labour, and my leisure too,
For his civility.

We passed the school where children played,
Their lessons scarcely done;
We passed the fields of gazing grain,
We passed the setting sun.

We paused before a house that seemed
A swelling of the ground;
The roof was scarcely visible,
The cornice but a mound.

Since then 'tis centuries; but each
Feels shorter than the day

I first surmised the horses' heads
Were toward eternity.

If the word 'great' means anything in poetry, this poem is one of the greatest in the English language; it is flawless to the last detail. The swift rhythm puts motion into the feeling of suspended action back of the poem. Every image is absolutely precise and is, moreover, not merely beautiful, but inextricably bound up with the central idea; every image extends and intensifies every other. The third stanza especially shows Miss Dickinson's power to fuse, in the same moment of perception, a heterogeneous series: the children, the grain, and the setting sun (infinity) have the same degree of credibility; the first subtly preparing for the last. The sharp *gazing* before *grain*, dominating the poem, makes sensuous the whole quality of suspended action. The content of Death in the poem eludes forever any explicit definition. He is a gentleman taking a lady out for a ride—but note the restraint that keeps the poet from carrying this so far that it is ludicrous and incredible; and note the subtly interfused erotic motive, which the idea of death has presented to every romantic poet, being itself interchangeable with death. The terror of death is rationalized through this figure of the genteel driver, who thus is made ironically to serve the end of Immortality. This is the heart of the poem: the poet knows that it is fiction; she has presented the typical puritan theme in all its final irresolution, without making any final statement about it. There is no solution to the problem, there can be only a statement of it in the full context of intellect and feeling. A construction of the human will, elaborated with all the abstracting powers of the mind, is put to the concrete test of experience; the idea of immortality is submitted to the fact of disintegration. We are not told what to think; we are told to look at the situation.

The framework of the poem is, in fact, the two abstractions, mortality and eternity, which are made to associate in perfect equality with the images: she sees the ideas, and thinks the perceptions. She did, of course, nothing of the sort; but we must use the logical distinctions, even to the extent of paradox, if we are to form any notion of this rare quality of mind. She could not in the proper sense think at all, and unless we prefer the feeble poetry of ideas that flourished in New England in the eighties, we must conclude that her intellectual deficiency was her greatest distinction. Miss Dickinson is probably the only Anglo-American poet of her century whose work exhibits the perfect literary situation—the fusion of feeling and thinking. Unlike her contemporaries, she never succumbed to her ideas, to easy solutions, to her private desires.

Philosophers must deal with ideas, but the trouble with most nineteenth-century poets is too much philosophy; they are nearer to being philosophers than poets, without being in the true sense either. Tennyson is a perfectly bad example of this; so is Arnold in his weak moments. There have been poets like Milton and Donne who were not spoiled for their true business by leaning on a rational system of ideas; that was because they understood their ideas. Tennyson tried to mix a little Huxley and a little Broad Church, without understanding either Broad Church or Huxley; the result was fatal, and what is worse, it was false and hollow. Miss Dickinson's ideas were deeply imbedded in her character, not taken from the latest tract. A conscious cultivation of ideas in poetry is always dangerous, and even Milton escaped ruin only by having an infallible instinct for what in the deepest sense he understood. Even at that there is a remote quality in Milton's approach to his material, in his treatment of it; in the nineteenth century, in an imperfect literary situation where literature was confused with documentation, he might have been a pseudo-philosopher-poet. It is impossible to conceive Emily Dickinson and John Donne ever becoming that; they would not have written at all.

Neither the feeling nor the style of Miss Dickinson belongs to the seventeenth century; yet between her and Donne there are remarkable ties. Their religious ideas, their abstractions, are momently toppling from the rational plane to the level of perception. The ideas, in fact, are no longer the impersonal religious ideas defined anew in the heat of emotion, that we find in poets like Herbert and Vaughan. They have become, for them, the terms of personality; they are mingled with the miscellany of sensation. In Miss Dickinson, as in Donne, there is a singularly morbid concern, not for religious truth, but for personal revelation. The modern word is self-exploitation. It is egoism grown irresponsible in religion, and decadent in morals. In religion it is blasphemy; in society it means usually that culture is not self-contained and sufficient, that the inner community is breaking up. This is, along with some other features that do not concern us here, the perfect literary situation.

II

Personal revelation of the kind that Donne and Miss Dickinson strove for, in the effort to understand their relation to the world, is a feature of all great poetry; it is probably the unconscious motive for writing. It is the unconscious effort of the individual to live apart from a cultural tradition that no longer sustains him. But this culture, which I now wish to discuss a little, is indispensable: there is a great deal of shallow nonsense in modern criticism which holds that poetry—and this is a half-truth that is wholly false—is essentially revolutionary. It is only indirectly revolutionary: the intellectual and religious background of an age no longer contains the whole spirit, and the poet proceeds to examine that background in experience. But the background is absolutely necessary; otherwise all the arts, not only poetry, would have to rise in a vacuum. Poetry does not dispense with tradition; it probes the deficiencies of a tradition. It is too bad that Arnold did not explain his doctrine, that poetry is a criticism of life, from the viewpoint of its background; we should have been spared an era of academic misconception, in which criticism meant a diluted pragmatism, the criterion of which was respectability. The poet in the true sense 'criticizes' his tradition, either as such, or indirectly by comparing it with something that is about to replace it; he does what the root-meaning of the verb implies—he *discerns* its real elements and thus establishes its value, by putting it to the test of experience.

What is the nature of such a culture? Or to put the question properly, what is the meaning of culture for poetry? All the great poets become the material of what we popularly call culture; we study them to acquire it. But it is clear that Addison was more cultivated than Shakespeare; nevertheless Shakespeare is a finer source of culture than Addison. What is the meaning of this? Plainly it is that learning has never had anything to do with culture except instrumentally: the poet must be exactly literate enough to write down fully and precisely what he has to say, but no more. The source of a poet's true culture lies back of all this, and not all the strenuous activity of this enlightened age can create it.

It cannot be consciously created. It is simply an available source of ideas that were imbedded in a complete and homogeneous society. The poet finds himself balanced upon the moment when such a world is about to fall, when it threatens to run out into looser and less self-sufficient impulses. This world order is assimilated, in Miss Dickinson, as medievalism was in Shakespeare, to the poetic vision; it is brought down from abstraction to personal feeling. Now in this connection it may be said that the prior conditions for great poetry, given a great talent, are just two: the thoroughness of the poet's discipline in a great objective system of 'truths,' and his lack of consciousness of such a discipline. For this discipline is a number of fundamental ideas the source of which the poet does not know; they give form and stability to his fresh perceptions of the world; and he cannot shake them off. This is his culture, and like Tennyson's God, it is nearer than hands and feet. With reasonable certainty we unearth the elements of Shakespeare's culture, and yet it is equally certain—so innocent was he of his own resources—that he would not know what our discussion is about. He appeared at the collapse of the mediaeval system as a rigid pattern of life, but that pattern remained in Shakespeare, and in all men, what Shelley called a "fixed point of reference" for their sensibilities. Miss Dickinson, as we have seen, was born into an equilibrium of an old and a new order. Puritanism could not be to her what it had been to the generation of Cotton Mather—a body of absolute truths; it was an unconscious discipline timed to the pulse of her life.

The perfect literary situation—that is what it is: it produces, because it is rare, a special and perhaps the most distinguished kind of poet. However, I am not trying to invent a new critical category; such poets are never very much alike on the surface; they show us all the varieties of poetic feeling; and like other poets they resist all classification but that of temporary convenience. But, I believe, Miss Dickinson and John Donne would have this in common: Their sense of the natural world is not shut off by a too rigid system of ideas; yet the ideas, the abstractions, their education or their intellectual heritage, are not so weak as to let their immersion in nature, or their purely personal quality, get out of control. The two poles of the mind are not separately visible; we infer them from their balanced activity. There is no thought as such at all; nor is there feeling; there is that unique product which is neither and both. It was the habit of the eighteenth century to go to Shakespeare—when it went to him at all—to see what he thought about morals, politics, religion. Shakespeare has no opinions whatever; his peculiar merit is deeply involved in his failure to think about anything; his meaning is not in the content of his expression; it is in the total relations of his characters. This kind of poetry is at the opposite of intellectualism. (Miss Dickinson is obscure and difficult, but that is not intellectualism.) To T. W. Higginson, the editor of the *Atlantic Monthly* who tried to advise her, she wrote that she had no education. In any sense that Higginson could understand, it was quite true. That kind of education is the conscious cultivation of abstractions. She did not reason about the world she saw; she merely saw it. The world within her rose up, concentrated in her slightest perception.

That kind of world at present has something of the fascination of archeology. There is none like it. When such worlds exist, when such cultures flourish, they support not only the poet but all members of society. For, from these, the poet differs only in his gift for exhibiting the structure, the internal lineaments, of his culture by threatening to tear them apart: a process that concentrates the typical emotions of society while it seems to attack them. The poet may hate his age; he may think that he is attacking it, as Dante did, or he may be an outcast like Villon; but his world is always there as the background to what he has to say. It is the lens through which he brings nature to focus and control—the clarifying medium that concentrates his personal feeling. It is ready-made; he cannot make it; with it, his poetry has a spontaneity and a certainty of direction that, without it, it would lack. No poet could have invented the elements of *The Chariot*; only a great poet could have used them so perfectly. Miss Dickinson was a deep mind writing from a deep culture, and when she came to poetry, she came infallibly, for "custom had made it in her a property of easiness."

Infallibly, at her best; for no poet has ever been perfect, neither is Emily Dickinson. Her unsurpassed precision of statement is due to the directness with which she applies the abstract framework of her thought to its unorganized material. The two elements of her style, considered as point of view, are immortality, or the idea of permanence, and the physical process of death or decay. Her diction has two corresponding features: words of Latin or Greek origin and, sharply opposed to these, the concrete Saxon element. It is this verbal conflict that gives to her verse its high tension; it is not a deliberately seized upon device, but a feeling for language that senses out the two fundamental components of English and their metaphysical relation: the Latin for ideas and the Saxon for perceptions—the peculiar virtue of English as a poetic tongue. Only the great poets know how to use this advantage of our language. Like all poets, Miss Dickinson often writes out of habit; the style that emerged from some deep exploration of an idea is carried on as verbal habit when she has nothing to say. She indulges herself:

> There's something quieter than sleep
> Within this inner room!
> It wears a sprig upon its breast,
> And will not tell its name.
>
> Some touch it and some kiss it,
> Some chafe its idle hand;
> It has a simple gravity
> I do not understand!
>
> While simple hearted neighbors
> Chat of the 'early dead,'
> We, prone to periphrasis,
> Remark that birds have fled!

It is only a pert remark; at best a superior kind of punning—one of the worst specimens of her occasional interest in herself. She never had the slightest interest in the public: were four poems, or was it five, published in her lifetime? She never felt the temptation to round off a poem for public exhibition. Higginson's polite attempt to make her verse 'correct' was an invitation to throw her work into the public ring—the ring of Lowell and Longfellow. He could not see that he was tampering with one of rarest literary integrities of all time. Here was a poet who had no use for the supports of authorship—flattery and fame; she never needed money.

She had all the elements of a culture that has broken up, a culture that on the religious side takes its place in the museum of spiritual antiquities. Puritanism, as a unified version of the world, is dead; only a remnant of it in trade can be said to survive. In the history of puritanism she comes between Hawthorne and Emerson. She has Hawthorne's matter, which a too irresponsible personality tends to dilute into a form like Emerson's; she is often betrayed by words. But she is not the poet of a personal sentiment; she has more to say than she can put down in any one poem. Like Hardy and Whitman she must be read entire; like Shakespeare she never gives up her meaning in a single line. She is therefore a perfect subject for the kind of criticism which is chiefly concerned with general ideas. She exhibits one of the permanent relations between personality and objective truth, and she deserves the special attention of our own time, which lacks that kind of truth.

She has Hawthorne's intellectual toughness, a hard, definite sense of the physical world. The highest flights to God, the most extravagant metaphors of the strange and the remote, come back to a point of casuistry, to a moral dilemma of the experienced world. There is, in spite of the homiletic vein of utterance, no abstract speculation, nor is there a message to society; she speaks wholly to individual experience. She offers to the unimaginative no riot of vicarious sensation; she has no useful maxims for men of action. Up to this point her resemblance to Emerson is slight: poetry is a sufficient form of utterance, and her devotion to it is pure. But in Emily Dickinson the puritan world is no longer self-contained; it is no longer complete, for her sensibility exceeds its dimensions. She has trimmed down its supernatural proportions; it has become a morality; instead of the tragedy of the spirit there is a commentary upon it. Her poetry is a magnificent personal confession, blasphemous and in its self-revelation, its implacable honesty, almost obscene. It comes out of an intellectual life towards which it feels no moral responsibility. Mather would have burnt her for a witch.

Chronology

1830	Emily Dickinson born in Amherst, Massachusetts, on December 10.
1835	Dickinson begins four years of Primary School.
1840	Dickinson starts first of seven years at Amherst Academy.
1847	Dickinson enters South Hadley Seminary.
1850	Amherst College student newspaper anonymously publishes a Dickinson valentine.
1855	Dickinson visits her father in Washington, D.C.; meets Charles Wadsworth; family moves into the Homestead.
1856	Austin Dickinson marries Susan Gilbert, and they move into the Evergreens.
1858	Austin Dickinson introduces Emily to Samuel Bowles, publisher of the *Springfield Republican.*
1861	*Springfield Republican* anonymously publishes "I taste a liquor never brewed" under the title "The May Wine."
1862	Dickinson sends a letter and four poems to Thomas Wentworth Higginson; *Springfield Republican* anonymously publishes "Safe in their alabaster chambers."
1864	Dickinson in Boston for eye treatments.

1865	*Springfield Republican* anonymously publishes "A narrow Fellow in the grass."
1870	Thomas Wentworth Higginson first visits Amherst.
1874	Dickinson's father dies suddenly in Boston.
1875	Dickinson's mother suffers a paralytic stroke.
1876	Helen Hunt Jackson urges Dickinson to publish.
1878	Dickinson and Judge Otis Phillips Lord begin exchange of love letters.
1882	Mabel Loomis Todd and Austin Dickinson begin love affair; Dickinson's mother dies.
1883	Gilbert (Gib) Dickinson dies; Emily and Susan Dickinson continue estrangement.
1884	Judge Lord dies; Dickinson's health declines.
1886	Dickinson dies on May 15; Lavinia discovers her sister's poems.
1890	The first of many volumes of Dickinson's poems is published, with Loomis and Higginson as editors.
1955	Thomas H. Johnson publishes three volumes of Emily Dickinson's poetry.
1958	Johnson and Theodora Ward as editors publish three volumes of *The Letters of Emily Dickinson.*

Works by Emily Dickinson

"I taste a liquor never brewed,"("The May Wine"), 1861

"Safe in their alabaster chambers," 1862

"A narrow Fellow in the grass," 1865

"Success Is Counted Sweetest," ca. 1875

Poems of Emily Dickinson, eds. Mabel Loomis Todd and Thomas Wentworth Higginson, 1890 (published posthumously)

The complete poems of Emily Dickinson, introduction by Martha Dickinson Bianchi, 1924 (published posthumously)

Letters of Emily Dickinson, 1958 (published posthumously)

The complete poems of Emily Dickinson, ed. Thomas Johnson, 1960 (published posthumously)

Works about Emily Dickinson

Barker, Wendy. *Lunacy of Light: Emily Dickinson and the Experience of Metaphor.* Carbondale: Southern Illinois University Press, 1987.

Bingham, Millicent Todd. *Ancestor's brocade; the literary debut of Emily Dickinson.* NY: Harper & Brothers, 1945.

———. *Emily Dickinson, a revelation.* NY: Harper, 1954.

———. Emily Dickinson's home; letters of Edward Dickinson and his family. With documentation and comment by Millicent Todd Bingham. NY: Harper, 1955.

Capps, Jack L. *Emily Dickinson's Reading, 1836-1886.* Cambridge, Mass.: Harvard University Press, 1966.

Clayton, Mark. "Everybody Loves Emily Dickinson," in *The Christian Science Monitor*, 12/21/99, p. 18.

Cody, John. *After Great Pain: The Inner Life of Emily Dickinson.* Cambridge, Mass.: Harvard University Press, 1971.

Dickie, Margaret. *Lyric Contingencies: Emily Dickinson and Wallace Stevens.* Philadelphia: University of Pennsylvania Press, 1991.

Diehl, Joanne F. *Dickinson and the Romantic Imagination.* Princeton, N.J.: Princeton University Press, 1981.

Eberwein, Jane Donahue, ed. *An Emily Dickinson Encyclopedia.* Westport, Conn.: Greenwood Press, 1998.

Farr, Judith. *The Passion of Emily Dickinson.* Cambridge: Harvard University Press, 1992.

Gelpi, Albert J. *Emily Dickinson: The Mind of a Poet.* Cambridge, Mass.: Harvard University Press, 1965.

Grabher, Gudrun, Roland Hagenbuchle, and Cristanne Miller, Eds. *The Emily Dickinson Handbook.* Amherst, Mass.: University of Massachusetts Press, 1998.

Gray, Janet. "Emily Dickinson," in *American Writers,* Retrospective Supplement, pp. 25-50. New York: Charles Scribner's Sons, 1998.

Hart, Ellen Louis, and Martha Nell Smith. *Open Me Carefully.* Ashfield, Mass.: Paris Press, 1998.

Johnson, Thomas H. ed. *The Poems of Emily Dickinson, including Variant Readings Critically Compared with All Known Manuscripts.* 3 vols. Cambridge: Harvard University Press, 1955.

———. ed. *The complete poems of Emily Dickinson.* Boston: Little, Brown, 1997.

———. ed. *Final harvest: Emily Dickinson's poems.* Boston: Little, Brown, 1997.

———. ed. *Emily Dickinson: Selected Letters,* 9th ed. Cambridge, Mass.: The Belknap Press, Harvard University Press, 1998.

Johnson, Thomas H., and Theodora Ward. eds. *The Letters of Emily Dickinson.* 3 vols. Cambridge: Harvard University Press, 1986.

Keller, Karl. *The Only Kangaroo Among the Beauty.* Baltimore: The Johns Hopkins Press, 1979.

Longsworth, Polly. *Emily Dickinson: Her Letter to the World.* New York: Thomas Y. Crowell Co., 1965.

———. *The World of Emily Dickinson.* New York: W. W. Norton & Company, 1990.

Luce, William. *The Belle of Amherst: A Play Based on the Life of Emily Dickinson.* Boston: Houghton-Mifflin, 1976.

Martin, Wendy. *An American Triptych: Anne Bradstreet, Emily Dickinson, Adrienne Rich.* Chapel Hill: University of North Carolina Press, 1984.

Miller, Ruth. *The poetry of Emily Dickinson.* Middletown, Connecticut: Wesleyan University Press, 1968.

Olsen, Victoria. *Emily Dickinson, Poet.* New York: Chelsea House Publishers, 1990.

Rich, Adrienne. "Vesuvius at Home: The Power of Emily Dickinson," in Sandra M. Gilbert and Susan Gubar, eds. *Shakespeare's Sisters: Feminist Essays on Women Poets*. Bloomington, Indiana: Indiana University Press, 1979.

Rosenbaum, S. P. ed. *A Concordance to the Poems of Emily Dickinson.* Ithaca: Cornell University Press, 1978.

Sewall, Richard B. "Teaching Dickinson: Testimony of a Veteran," in *Approaches to Teaching Emily Dickinson*. Modern Language Association, 1989.

———. *The Life of Emily Dickinson*, 2 vols. Cambridge, Mass.: Harvard University Press, 1980.

Smith, Robert M. *The Seductions of Emily Dickinson.* Tuscaloosa: University of Alabama Press, 1996.

Whicher, George F. *This Was a Poet: A Critical Biography of Emily Dickinson*. New York: Scribner's, 1938.

Wolff, Cynthia Griffin. *Emily Dickinson*. New York: Alfred A. Knopf, 1986.

Wolosky, Shira. *Emily Dickinson: A Voice of War.* New Haven: Yale University Press, 1984.

Websites

The Academy of American Poets – Emily Dickinson
www.poets.org/poets/edick

Dickinson Electronic Archives
www.iath.virginia.edu/dickinson/

The Dickinson Homestead
www.dickinsonhomestead.org/index.html

The Emily Dickinson International Society
www.cwru.edu/affil/edis/edisindex.html

Virtual Emily
www-unix.oit.umass.edu/~emilypg/1813.html

Contributors

HAROLD BLOOM is Sterling Professor of the Humanities at Yale University and Henry W. and Albert A. Berg Professor of English at the New York University Graduate School. He is the author of over 20 books, including *Shelley's Mythmaking* (1959), *The Visionary Company* (1961), *Blake's Apocalypse* (1963), *Yeats* (1970), *A Map of Misreading* (1975), *Kabbalah and Criticism* (1975), *Agon: Toward a Theory of Revisionism* (1982), *The American Religion* (1992), *The Western Canon* (1994), and *Omens of Millennium: The Gnosis of Angels, Dreams, and Resurrection* (1996). *The Anxiety of Influence* (1973) sets forth Professor Bloom's provocative theory of the literary relationships between the great writers and their predecessors. His most recent books include *Shakespeare: The Invention of the Human*, a 1998 National Book Award finalist, and *How to Read and Why*, which was published in 2000. In 1999, Professor Bloom received the prestigious American Academy of Arts and Letters Gold Medal for Criticism.

KAY CORNELIUS is a former English teacher who resides in Huntsville, Alabama. She has studied Dickinson's poems and has taught them to her students over the years. This is her fifth book for Chelsea House.

SANDRA McCHESNEY is Professor of English at Pennsylvania State University at DuBois. She is a member of the Learning Center Team.

ADRIENNE RICH is the recipient of the 1996 Tanning Award for Mastery in the Art of Poetry, as well as the Lannan Foundation's 1999 Lifetime Achievement Award. She is the author of more than fifteen volumes of poetry, including *Diving into the Wreck* and *The Dream of a Common Language*. Her most recent book of essays is entitled: *Arts of the Possible: Essays & Conversations* (2001).

A poet and a scholar, ALLEN TATE was Professor of English at the University of Minnesota. His works include *Mr. Pope and Other Poems*, *Collected Poems*, and *Reactionary Essays on Poetry and Ideas*.

Index